Inner Strength
for Active Apostles

Dom Jean-Baptiste Chautard

Inner Strength
for Active Apostles

How to Win Souls
Without Losing Your Own

SOPHIA INSTITUTE PRESS®
Manchester, New Hampshire

Inner Strength for Active Apostles is a slightly abridged version of *The True Apostolate*, third edition (St. Louis: B. Herder Book Company, 1925). This 2003 edition by Sophia Institute Press includes minor editorial revisions and uses the term *apostle* in place of *apostolic laborer* and *apostolic worker*.

Sophia Institute Press®
Box 5284, Manchester, NH 03108
1-800-888-9344
www.sophiainstitute.com

Nihil obstat: F. G. Holweck, *Censor Librorum*
St. Louis, May 29, 1918
Imprimatur: Joannes J. Glennon, Archbishop of St. Louis
St. Louis, May 30, 1918

Library of Congress Cataloging-in-Publication Data

Chautard, J. B. (Jean Baptiste), 1858-1935.
    Inner strength for active Apostles : how to win souls without losing your own / Jean-Baptiste Chautard.
        p. cm.
    Includes bibliographical references.
    ISBN 1-928832-94-6 (pbk. : alk. paper)
    1. Spiritual life — Catholic authors. I. Title.
BX2182.3 .C47 2003
248.4'82 — dc22   2003021550

03 04 05 06 07 08 09 10 9 8 7 6 5 4 3 2 1

Contents

Preface

This work of Dom Jean-Baptiste Chautard, Trappist Abbot of Sept-Fons, is specially destined to benefit all persons who are regularly engaged in laboring for the salvation of souls, either directly or indirectly, in the works of both spiritual and corporal mercy. On account of its solid doctrine and wise and practical directions and counsels, it has been praised by Pope Benedict XV and recommended to the clergy and the religious by Pope Pius X, many cardinals, and numerous bishops. Published in 1912, it obtained so great a success that, four years later, in 1916, it had reached its sixth edition, and fifty thousand copies had already been sold.

We hope that this valuable work, although somewhat condensed in its English dress, will prove profitable to the apostles of our country and of other English-speaking countries. To realize this hope, we unite with its pious and learned author in offering this little work to the Blessed Virgin Mary.

O Mary Immaculate,
Queen of Apostles,
deign to bless
these modest pages,

and obtain that all their readers
may fully understand that,
if God is pleased to make use of them
as regular instruments of His Providence,
for dispensing heavenly goods
to the souls of their fellowmen,
they, on their part, should endeavor,
by their virtues and holy life,
to be intimately united to
Jesus Christ, their Model.
O Mary, Mother of God
and our Mother also,
bless us and our
apostolic labors. Amen.

Inner Strength
for Active Apostles

God desires apostolic works as well as apostolic zeal

To the divine nature pertains sovereign liberality. Goodness tends to diffuse itself and to impart to others the good it enjoys.

The mortal life of our divine Savior was but a continual manifestation of His inexhaustible liberality. The Gospel shows Him sowing, on His way, treasures of love from His Heart, full of eagerness to draw mankind to the truth and the life.

Our loving Redeemer communicated this flame of the apostolate to His Church as the gift of His love, the manifestation of His truth, and the resplendent reflection of His holiness. The mystical Spouse of Christ, animated with the same spirit, continues through succeeding ages the work of the apostolate of her divine Spouse and Model.

How admirable is the universal law established by Divine Providence, that man should learn the way of salvation through the ministry of man. "It pertains," says Pope Leo XIII, "to the ordinary law, by which God, who best provides for all things, has decreed that men should be saved mostly through men." Jesus Christ alone shed the Blood that redeemed the world. He could have applied its virtue Himself and have alone acted directly on men's souls, as He actually does in the blessed Eucharist. But He preferred to choose cooperators among men for dispensing His benefits. And why? Without doubt it was because the Divine Majesty would have it so. But besides, He was moved to do this by His tender love for men. And if it is befitting for the ruler of a state to govern chiefly through his ministers, it is nevertheless a wonderful condescension on the part of God to associate poor creatures, like ourselves, to His labors and glory.

The Church, born on the Cross from the pierced side of the Savior, perpetuates by the apostolic ministry the beneficent and redeeming action of the Man-God. This ministry, willed by Jesus Christ, becomes the essential factor for propagating the Church throughout the nations, and the ordinary instruments of her conquests.

In the first rank are the clergy, whose hierarchy forms the framework of the army of Jesus Christ, the clergy illustrated by so many holy and zealous bishops and priests, so gloriously honored of late by the beatification of the Curé d'Ars.[1]

Alongside the official clergy there arose, from the very beginning of Christianity, companies of volunteers, real *"corps d'elite,"* for special work, whose perpetual and luxuriant vegetation will always be one of the most manifest phenomena of the vitality of the Church.

First, in the early ages of the Church, came the contemplative orders, whose unceasing prayer and severe austerities so powerfully contributed to the conversion of the pagan world. In the Middle Ages, the preaching orders arose together with the mendicant and military orders and those devoted to the redemption of

---

[1] St. John Vianney (1786-1859), patron saint of parish priests. He was canonized in 1925, several years after this book was written.

the captive Christians from among infidel nations. And lastly, the modern times have beheld the birth and labors of numerous teaching orders, missionary institutes, congregations, and societies devoted to the care and relief of every kind of misfortune, need, and disease to which mankind is subject, whether spiritual or corporal.

Moreover, at every epoch of her history, the Church has found among the laity of both sexes numerous coworkers with her clergy and religious, such as fervent Catholics in every condition and state of life, who are now legion — men of action, as we may call them, ardent souls, who, uniting their forces and means in pious associations, place in the service of our Mother the Church their time, their talents, their means, and often even sacrifice their liberty and their life.

It is indeed an admirable and encouraging sight to behold the providential budding forth and blooming of apostolic activities, at the very time they are most needed, and so wonderfully adapted to the wants of the period, as is proven by the history of the Church. Every new want, every new danger to ward off or overcome invariably beholds the appearance of the institution required by the wants of the hour.

Hence, in our times we have beheld and still behold works, scarcely even thought of previously, arising around us to combat new evils, to fill new wants, such as laymen's retreats, Catholic societies and clubs for various timely purposes, the Apostleship of Prayer, the Work of the Propagation of the Faith, the Holy Childhood, the Association of the Catholic Press, the Total Abstinence Societies, the Holy Name Society, the Federation of Catholic Societies, and other works, of both local and general usefulness. All these are forms of the apostolate raised up by the spirit that inflamed the soul of St. Paul: "I most gladly will spend and be spent myself for your souls,"[2] and which seeks to spread everywhere the benefits of the Blood of our Redeemer, Jesus Christ.

The object of these works of the apostolate is threefold: first, to win souls or preserve them to Jesus Christ; secondly, to promote the spiritual welfare of the apostles; and thirdly, to please God and promote His glory. However noble and meritorious these apostolic works are in themselves, the apostles should constantly watch over themselves, for these very works, if not properly performed, will not attain this threefold object, but may even prove danger-ous to the laborers themselves. Wherefore, it behooves them to imitate the great Apostle St. Paul, who strove to perform the la-bors of his apostolate properly, "lest, when I have preached to oth-ers, I myself should become a castaway."[3]

Our object in writing this book has been to indicate to apostles the chief means requisite for attaining the threefold object of their apostolate.

---

[2] 2 Cor. 12:15. Biblical quotations are taken from the Douay-Rheims edition of the Old and New Testaments. Where appli-cable, quotations have been cross-referenced with the differing names and enumeration in the Revised Standard Version, using the following symbol: (RSV =).

[3] 1 Cor. 9:27.

Part One

The apostle must develop his interior life

Chapter One

Jesus should be the life of all apostolic works

Modern science has reason to be proud of its immense progress and success. There is, however, one thing that has hitherto been and shall forever be impossible for it to perform — namely, to create life, to produce from a chemist's laboratory a grain of wheat, a larva, a worm. The celebrated Pasteur has completely defeated the arguments of the advocates of "spontaneous generation" and has proved the futility and error of such pretentious theories. God has reserved *to Himself* the power to create life.

In the vegetable and animal kingdoms, living beings can increase and multiply, but their fecundity depends on the conditions laid down by the Creator. But as to intellectual life, God reserves it to Himself and *directly* creates the rational soul. Furthermore, there is a far higher domain, of which He is still more jealous: the domain of the supernatural life, for it is an emanation of the divine life communicated to the human nature of the Incarnate Word.

"Through Jesus Christ our Lord; with Him and in Him." The Incarnation and the Redemption establish Jesus as the Source, the only Source, of this divine life, in which all men are called to participate. The essential action of the Church consists in spreading this supernatural life among mankind by means of the sacraments, prayer, preaching, and all the works connected therewith.

The heavenly Father does nothing except through His Son, for "all things have been made by Him, and without Him was nothing made that was made."[4] This is true in the natural order, but how much more in the supernatural order, in which God communicates His intimate life to men and "renders them partakers of the divine nature," in order to make them "children of God."[5]

"I came that they might have life"; "In Him was life"; "I am the life."[6] How precise are these words! How luminous is the parable of the vine and the branches, in which our divine Master develops this truth![7] And how He insists thereon, in order to engrave deeply in the minds of His Apostles the fundamental principle that *He*, Jesus, alone is the Life, and the consequence of this principle: that in order to *participate* in this life and communicate it to others, they should be grafted onto the Man-God.

They who are called to be coworkers with the Savior in transmitting to souls this divine life should, therefore, consider themselves as mere channels charged with drawing this life from its original and only source.

An apostle who would disregard these principles, and imagine that of himself he can produce the slightest vestige of the supernatural life without receiving it all from Jesus, would be guilty of a theological error.

Moreover, the apostle who, through blind presumption, would, in his functions, rely chiefly on his own efforts and work, rather

---

[4] John 1:3.
[5] 2 Pet. 1:4; cf. 1 John 3:1.
[6] John 10:10; 1:4; 14:6.
[7] John 15.

than on Jesus Christ, would be very displeasing to God on account of such presumption. Let us bear in mind that the apostle has only a secondary and subordinate role to fill, and that all his labors and talents cannot produce real fruit without divine grace and blessing, for our divine Savior tells us expressly, "Without me you can do nothing."[8] And St. Paul declares the same in other words, saying, "I have planted, Apollo watered, but God gave the increase. Therefore, neither he that planteth is anything, nor he that watereth, but God that giveth the increase."[9] Let us always bear in mind that in all that concerns the spiritual life, either in ourselves or in others, we are powerless of ourselves, and that all "our sufficiency is from God."[10]

[8] John 15:5.
[9] 1 Cor. 3:6-7.
[10] 2 Cor. 3:5.

Chapter Two

Developing an interior life means nurturing the life of Christ within you

When, in the course of these pages, we use words found in the works of the Fathers, the Scholastics, and ascetical writers such as *life of mental prayer, contemplation*, and *contemplative life*, we always mean the very interior life accessible to all, and not the unusual states of mental prayer treated in mystic theology, and especially not ecstasies, visions, raptures, and the like. Nor is the study of asceticism our object. We shall here limit ourselves to recall briefly certain truths that all who wish to care properly for their soul are bound to accept.

    • *First truth:* The supernatural life is the very life of Jesus Christ Himself in me by faith, hope, and charity.

This presence of our Lord by the supernatural life is not His Real Presence peculiar to Holy Communion, but a presence by vital action, like the action of the head or the heart on the members, an intimate presence that God usually conceals from my soul to increase the merit of my faith; wherefore this action is habitually imperceptible to my natural faculties. Such action does not interfere with my free will and utilizes events, persons, and things to enable me to know the will of God and to profit by the occasions of acquiring or increasing my participation in the divine life. This life, inaugurated at Baptism by the state of grace, perfected by Confirmation, and supported and nourished by the Eucharist, is my Christian life.

• *Second truth:* By this life, Jesus Christ imparts His Spirit to me and thereby becomes the superior principle, if I place no obstacle, and moves me to think, judge, love, will, suffer, and work with Him, in Him, through Him, and like Him. My external actions then become the manifestations of the life of Jesus in me. In this manner do I tend to realize the ideal of the interior life thus formulated by St. Paul: "I live, now not I, but Christ liveth in me."[11]

There is no essential difference between the terms *Christian life, piety, interior life,* and *holiness,* for they are only diverse degrees of one and the same love; they are like the twilight, the dawn, the light, and the splendor of one and the same sun. My interior life will be my Christian life blooming in the normal development that God expected of me when granting me the grace of Baptism. If I am a priest or a religious, I am still more obliged to cultivate this life. It consists essentially in purity of heart and generosity of life, and may be defined as a habitual and always more and more exact, strong, and extended custody of the heart, which, by frequent recourse to God, arms us for our daily strife against our defects, enables us to acquire the virtues, and by uniting our soul to Jesus, perfects us in divine love.

By the custody of my heart, my soul, like a watchful sentinel, is not only constantly armed against all attacks from the seven capital sins, but is always attentive to all interior motives and

---

[11] Gal. 2:20.

competent to regulate my conduct by the Spirit of Jesus and in accordance with my duty. How far my interior life is connected with the custody of the heart is shown by these words of Holy Writ: "With all watchfulness keep thy heart, because life issueth out of it."[12]

• *Third truth:* I would lack one of the most powerful means of acquiring the interior life if I did not strive to possess a precise and sure belief in the active presence of Jesus within me, and did not exert myself so that such a presence should become in me a living reality, penetrating more and more the atmosphere of my faculties. In this manner, Jesus will become my light, my ideal, my counsel, my support, my recourse, my strength, my Physician, my consolation, my joy, my love — in short, my life — and I shall then be able to acquire all the virtues. And I shall then be able also to make truly my own the admirable prayer of St. Bonaventure[13] which the Church proposes to me as a thanksgiving after Mass, and begins with the words *"Transfige, dulcissime Domine Jesu"* ("Pierce, most sweet Lord Jesus").

• *Fourth truth:* In proportion to the intensity of my love of God, my supernatural life can increase every moment by a fresh infusion of the grace of the active presence of Jesus in me, produced whenever I perform meritorious acts, such as, practicing a virtue, working, suffering in its various forms, enduring privations and humiliations, practicing self-denial, praying, hearing Mass, performing acts of devotion to our Lady, and receiving the sacraments, especially the Holy Eucharist.

---

[12] Prov. 4:23.

[13] St. Bonaventure (1221-1274), Franciscan mystical theologian and scholastic, writer, bishop, and Doctor.

O Jesus, this fact overpowers me
by its sublimity and depth,
but it especially fills me with joy and courage,
because by every occurrence, person, or thing,
Thou, O Jesus, objectively presentest
Thyself to me at every moment.
Under these appearances Thou concealest
Thy wisdom and Thy love,
and solicitest my cooperation,
in order to increase Thy life in me.

O my soul, it is Jesus who presents Himself
to thee by the grace of the present moment,
prompting me to say a prayer, to say or hear Mass,
to do spiritual reading, or to make an act of patience,
zeal, self-denial, resistance to temptation, confidence,
or love. Wouldst thou reject such an inspiration?

• *Fifth truth:* The threefold concupiscence arising from Original Sin, and intensified by my actual sins, places within me elements of spiritual death opposed to the life of Jesus and, in proportion as they are developed, diminish its activity and may even extinguish it altogether. Nevertheless, all inclinations and sentiments opposed to this life of Jesus in me, and even violent and protracted temptations, can do me no harm, so long as my will is opposed to their assaults. How consoling it is to reflect that temptations, like every element of spiritual combat, serve to increase in me the life of Jesus in proportion to my zeal in overcoming them.

• *Sixth truth:* If I neglect to use faithfully the appropriate means, my mind will become blind and my will too weak to cooperate with Jesus in increasing and sustaining in me this life. Thence follows a progressive diminution of His life in me, and my path will be directed toward tepidity of will.[14] Through dissipation, sloth, illusion, or blindness, I live in peace with venial sin, and therefore I am not secure of salvation, because tepidity easily disposes to mortal sin. If I were unfortunate enough to fall into tepidity, or even still lower, I should make every exertion to recover true fervor, first, by reflecting more seriously on my own death as near, on judgment, Hell, eternity, and the enormity of sin; secondly, by reflecting lovingly, O Jesus, on Thy sacred wounds, going to Calvary in spirit and prostrating myself at Thy feet, so that Thy precious living Blood falling upon me might dissipate my blindness, melt my icy soul, and shake the torpor off my weak will.

• *Seventh truth:* I should be in dread of not possessing interior life in the degree Jesus requires of me, first, if my desire to live by Jesus, to please Him, and my dread of displeasing Him in the least cease to grow; if I no longer make use of the necessary means, such as prayer, the particular and the general examination of conscience,

---

[14] There are three kinds of tepidity. There is tepidity of mere feeling, as when we feel spiritually dry at prayer, and it will prove beneficial, if we try to overcome it. There is tepidity of frailty, that is, committing faults but not deliberately, and only out of mere human frailty — such faults are not dangerous. And there is tepidity of the will. He who has fallen into tepidity of the will commits venial faults deliberately, habitually, and makes no serious effort to correct them. He wishes, indeed, to save his soul, but is not willing to make the necessary efforts or exertions, for he is too fond of his ease and comfort; he is willing to avoid mortal sin, but makes no account of venial sins and commits them without remorse. It is as if he said to God, "I will avoid only the sins that are deserving of Hell; as to the others, I do not care how many I commit or how often I displease Thee." This tepidity leads to mortal sin.

spiritual reading, and reception of the sacraments; or, if through my own fault, I draw no profit therefrom. Secondly, if in my occupations, I do not practice the minimum of recollection requisite to enable me to keep my heart in the purity and generosity sufficient to keep the voice of Jesus from being stifled, when it warns me of the dangers besetting my path and urges me to combat them. This minimum will be wanting to me if I neglect the means of securing it, such as leading a liturgical life, raising my heart to God by the practice of brief, spontaneous prayers, petitions, spiritual communions, the presence of God, and good intentions.

Without God's assistance, venial sins will soon swarm in my life, even if I should not be aware of it. To screen them and to conceal from me a state even more lamentable, the illusion will make use of an appearance of piety, more theoretical than practical, and of zeal for the apostolic works. My blindness in this matter will be rightly imputed to me, for having neglected to practice the necessary recollection.

• *Eighth truth:* Jesus Christ reigns in the soul who strives earnestly and lovingly to imitate Him in all things. There are two degrees in this imitation. In the first, the soul endeavors to acquire a holy indifference toward creatures in themselves, without reference to his own natural likes and dislikes, seeking in them, after the example of the Savior, only the will of God: "I came down from Heaven, not to do my will, but the will of Him that sent me."[15] Secondly, "Christ," says St. Paul, "did not please Himself."[16] In the second degree, the soul seeks preferably that which is repugnant to him, than that which is pleasant. To him who imitates the

---

[15] John 6:38.
[16] Rom. 15:3.

Savior's poverty and His love of sufferings and humiliations, and does violence to his merely natural feelings, these words of St. Paul may be rightly applied: "You have learned Christ."[17]

⋅ *Ninth truth:* In whatever state of life I am placed, if I really wish to pray and be faithful to divine grace, Jesus offers me all the means necessary to lead an interior life, to possess His friendship and make progress therein. This will make me cheerful and happy even in the midst of trials; and the words of Isaiah will be realized in me: "Then shall thy light break forth as the morning, and thy health shall speedily arise, and thy justice shall go before thy face, and the glory of the Lord shall gather thee up. Then shalt thou call, and the Lord shall hear . . . and the Lord will give thee rest, and will fill thy soul with brightness."[18]

⋅ *Tenth truth:* If God demands of me that I should direct my action, not merely to my own sanctification, but also to apostolic works, I will, before all, impress this firm conviction deeply in my soul: "Jesus shall be, as He demands, the life of all my apostolic labors." My own efforts in themselves are nothing, absolutely nothing, for Jesus says expressly, "Without me you can do nothing." My labors will prove useful and be blessed by God, provided that I, by my interior life, unite them to the vivifying action of Jesus Christ. Then, and then only, will they become all-powerful, for "I can do all things in Him who strengtheneth me."[19] Were I to labor from pride, self-confidence, or a selfish desire of success, God would reject all I do, for it would then be a sacrilegious folly on my part to endeavor to rob God of His glory for my own adornment! The

---

[17] Cf. Eph. 4:20.
[18] Isa. 58:8-9, 11.
[19] Phil. 4:13.

conviction of my own impotence, far from making me pusillani-
mous, will be a means of strength, for it will make me aware of the
necessity of prayer to obtain humility, which is a treasure for my
soul, the assurance of the divine help and the sure pledge of the
success of my labors.

When this "creed" of the interior life has become the foundation of its existence in us, it secures for us already in this life a
participation of heavenly happiness, because the interior life is indeed the life of the predestined and corresponds to the end for
which God has created us. It corresponds, moreover, to the Incarnation, for "God sent His only-begotten Son into the world, that
we may live by Him."[20] It is a blessed state, for, says St. Thomas,
"The end of man is to adhere to God, because in this his happiness
consists."[21]

Contrary to earthly joys, its thorns are all outward, but its roses
subsist inwardly. "How greatly are the worldly-minded to be pit-
ied!" exclaims the Curé d'Ars. "On their shoulders they wear a
cloak lined with sharp thorns, and they cannot make the least
movement without feeling their stings; but the true Christians
wear garments lined with soft skins." "Worldlings," says St. Bernard,[22] "see our crosses, indeed, but not the unction accompanying
them."

It is a heavenly state, and our soul becomes, as it were, a living
heaven. "Be always mindful of God," says St. Ephrem,[23] "and thy
mind will become a heaven to thee." And thy soul will chant with

---

[20] 1 John 4:9.

[21] St. Thomas Aquinas (1225-1274; Dominican philosopher, theologian, and Doctor), *Summa Theologica*, I-II, Q. 2, art. 8.

[22] St. Bernard of Clairvaux (1090-1153), abbot and Doctor.

[23] St. Ephrem (c. 306-373), theologian, preacher, Doctor, and writer
of poems, hymns, and biblical commentaries.

Blessed Margaret Mary,[24] "At all times and in all places, I will bear within me the God of my heart and the Heart of my God." "This is," says St. Thomas, "as a beginning of beatitude," and divine grace is Heaven in germ.

The interior life is often misunderstood. Pope St. Gregory,[25] who was as able an administrator and zealous an apostle as he was a great contemplative, briefly described the soul of St. Benedict,[26] when he was laying the foundation of his order, which became one of the greatest apostolic works on earth, in these words: "Benedict lived within himself." In our times, to live within oneself, to undertake to govern oneself, and not to allow oneself to be governed by external circumstances, to subject one's imagination, feelings, mind, and memory to one's will, and one's will entirely to the holy will of God, is a proceeding always less and less acceptable, for the new ideal is now, "Love of action for its own sake." To elude the discipline of subordination and subjection of one's faculties to the divine will, all mere pretexts are considered good, such as business, family cares, hygiene, popularity, love of country, prestige of the order or association, and a pretended glory of God; all vie with each other to keep us from living with or in ourselves. This sort of mania of living out of ourselves is apt to become an invisible attraction for us. Need we then wonder that the interior of life is not only misunderstood, but even sometimes despised and ridiculed, and this by certain persons who ought to appreciate its advantages

[24] St. Margaret Mary Alacoque (1647-1690), Visitation nun who received revelations of and promoted devotion to the Sacred Heart of Jesus. She was canonized in 1920, several years after this book was written.

[25] St. Gregory I (d. 604), Pope from 590, writer, and Doctor.

[26] St. Benedict (c. 480-c. 547), abbot who founded the monastery of Monte Cassino.

and necessity, so that Pope Leo XIII in one of his letters found it necessary to protest against the dangerous consequences of an exclusive admiration for apostolic works.

In order to avoid the very arduous labor required for leading a truly interior life, some go so far as practically to disparage "the life with Jesus, in Jesus, and through Jesus," and to ignore that in the divine plan of the Redemption everything is as truly based on the eucharistic life as on the Rock of Peter. To relegate that which is essential to a secondary place is what the disparagers of the interior life are unconsciously tending to effect. In their estimation, Holy Communion is no longer essential for themselves or for their apostolic labors. There are even some engaged in apostolic works who speak of their exploits as if the Almighty stood in need of their assistance.

Let us, however, bear in mind that just as God wishes only for "adorers in spirit and in truth,"[27] so also He wishes for "laborers in spirit," who labor, not so much for exterior results, for their own satisfaction, but solely to please and glorify God. God is pleased with the gifts of "His friends," of those who are "filled with His Spirit." He seeks first our heart, that is, our interior life; and if we give Him not our heart, no work of ours deserves His blessing. If the apostolic labors of those who lack the interior life are blessed with spiritual fruits, with success, it is owing, not so much to such a laborer's work or ability, as to the prayers and good works offered by persons truly pious, and, in certain cases, to the goodwill of the recipients of the divine favors, for the apostle in these cases is a mere instrument of the good effected.

The interior life, far from being an easy life, is really a very laborious life. It is a source of devotedness, of incomparable activity.

---

[27] John 4:23.

Because it is the more direct road to Heaven, the saying of Jesus Christ that the kingdom of Heaven suffereth violence, and the violent bear it away,[28] is applied to it in a special manner.

Dom Sebastian Wyart, who knew, by his varied experience, the labors of the ascetic, the fatigues of the military, and the cares of a great business, was fond of speaking of these three kinds of labor: the almost exclusive physical labor, such as farming, mechanics, and soldiering, he said, "is the easiest kind of work." Secondly, the intellectual work of the learned, the philosopher, the writer, the professor, the diplomat, the merchant, or the general in very active war is far more arduous and wears out more one's physical strength; it is like the sword-blade wearing out its scabbard. Thirdly, the labor requisite for leading an interior life is the most arduous of all when earnestly performed, for, says St. Gregory, "It is far more arduous to resist our vices and lusts than to engage in corporeal labors," but at the same time, it is the most consoling on earth, and almost the most important. It does more than a man's profession, for it forms man himself. How many engaged in the first two kinds of labor, which lead to fortune and success, glory in their courage, but are only sloth and cowardice when they have to labor to acquire virtue!

The aim of those who are determined to lead an interior life is to strive with all their energy constantly to govern themselves and their surroundings, so as to act in all things for the glory of God. To realize this object, they must endeavor in all circumstances to remain united to Jesus Christ and to concentrate their thoughts on the end to be attained and to weigh all they do by the light of the Gospel, repeating with St. Ignatius, "Whither am I going, and for what?" Wherefore everything in them, intellect and will, as well

[28] Matt. 11:12.

as memory, feelings, imagination, and senses, depends wholly on this one principle. But how great is the labor required to accomplish this result! Whether we mortify ourselves or allow ourselves some pleasure or enjoyment, whether we reflect or act, whether we work or rest, whether we love that which is good, or experience aversion or repugnance to that which is evil, whether we desire or fear, whether we accept joy or sadness, whether we hope or dread, whether we feel indignant or calm, we must persistently, always and in all things, direct ourselves according to God's holy will and good pleasure.

At prayer, especially before the Blessed Sacrament, we have to isolate ourselves still more completely from exterior objects, in order to be able to commune with the invisible God as if we actually beheld Him. "As seeing Him that is invisible."[29] Even in the midst of our apostolic labors, we should seek to realize the ideal that St. Paul so greatly admired in Moses. Neither the adversities of this life, or the storms of his passions, nor anything else can cause the interior man to deviate in the least from his line of conduct. If, however, he happens to falter or weaken therein for a moment, he soon recovers and resumes his progress with greater vigor than before.

And how arduous his labor! And how naturally we can understand that God already here below rewards, with special delights, those who do not grow faint from the efforts required for such a work. From which Dom Sebastian concludes, "Let the busiest of worldlings tell us whether their labors are as arduous as the labors required to lead a truly interior life! And who has not already experienced this? Often we priests and religious feel we would rather spend many hours in the most fatiguing bodily or

---

[29] Heb. 11:27.

mental labor than devote half an hour to a well-performed mental prayer, to devoutly hearing Mass or attentively reciting the Divine Office."

"Whatever be the difficulties of the active life," says an experienced Benedictine, "only those who lack experience venture to question or deny the arduous trials of the interior life. Many who are engaged in the active ministry admit that the hardest of all their duties is not working in the ministry, but performing the prescribed exercise of mental prayer, and that it is a relief for them to be called away from that exercise, in order to attend to some active duty of the ministry."

Father Faber regrets being obliged to admit that a quarter of an hour's thanksgiving after Mass or Communion is the most trying and tiresome quarter of an hour of the whole day. How disagreeable and repugnant to not a few is a short retreat of three days! To give up for only three days the comparatively easy, although very busy active life, and to live a few days in a supernatural atmosphere by infiltrating it into all the details of one's life, to compel one's mind to look at everything only with the eyes of faith, and to constrain one's heart to forget all, in order to inhale only Jesus and His life; to have a private interview with oneself, in order to discover one's spiritual infirmities and weaknesses, and to place one's soul without pity into a crucible to discover its faults! Such is the perspective that discourages many persons from leading the interior life who are equal to any amount of work and fatigue in merely natural or exterior objects. And if three such days appear so disagreeable, so trying, what does poor human nature experience at the idea of a whole life gradually trained in the exercises of the interior life!

There is no doubt that in this work of spiritual transformation, divine grace has a large share and renders "the yoke sweet and the burden light."[30] But, at the same time, how many and how great are the efforts demanded of each one's soul! How much does it cost one to get back into the right way and proceed until we can truly say, "Our conversation is in Heaven"?[31] "Man," says St. Thomas, "is placed between earthly objects and spiritual good, in which eternal beatitude consists; the closer he adheres to the one, the further he is removed from the other." When one end of the scale rises, the other goes down.

The catastrophe of Original Sin, having upset the economy of our being, renders this up-and-down motion of the scale very difficult to us. To reestablish and preserve, by means of the interior life, the original equilibrium of man's little world is very difficult. There is need of much labor, trouble, and sacrifice, for a crumbled edifice has to be rebuilt and preserved from a fresh ruin. Hence, how arduous the task of constantly tearing away from earthly thoughts and aspirations, by dint of watchfulness, self-denial, and mortification, that heart of ours, which is borne down by the immense weight of our corrupt nature — to reform our character especially in those points which render it so unlike the physiognomy of our Savior's soul, since we are so dissipated in mind, passionate, self-complacent, proud, harsh, devoid of higher motives, selfish, unkind; to resist the allurements of present and sensible pleasure by the hope of a spiritual happiness, which can be enjoyed only after an indefinitely long expectation; to detach ourselves from all that may attach to this earth, and to make an unreserved holocaust of all attachment to creatures, of all merely natural desires, aspirations, lusts, and external good, and of our self-will and judgment. How great a task!

---

[30] Cf. Matt. 11:30.
[31] Phil. 3:20.

Nurturing the life of Christ within you

And yet this is only the preparatory or the purifying part of the interior life. That close, intimate struggle caused St. Paul to make the following avowal: "I am delighted with the law of God according to the inward man. But I see another law in my members fighting against the law of my mind and captivating me in the law of sin, which is in my members. Unhappy man that I am, who shall deliver me from the body of this death?"[32]

The celebrated Father Ravignan, S.J., speaking on this very subject, said, "You ask me what I did during my novitiate. There were two of us; I pitched one of them out of the window, and I alone remained."

After this struggle without truce with a foe ever ready to rise up again, it behooves us to protect ourselves against the least return of the natural spirit into our heart; for after having been purified by penance, it is now consumed by the desire of repairing the outrages committed against God, of using its whole energy to strive to acquire the invisible beauty of the virtues of Jesus Christ by faithful imitation and absolute confidence in Divine Providence. In this consists the labor of acquiring the interior life itself. How great the field of labor required to do this!

The labor must be intimate, assiduous, and constant. By its means, the soul acquires a wonderful facility and an astonishing rapidity of execution in performing apostolic labors. This secret belongs exclusively to the interior life.

The immense works accomplished, in spite of poor health, by Sts. Augustine, John Chrysostom, Bernard, Thomas Aquinas, and Vincent de Paul[33] are really astonishing. And what is still more

---

[32] Rom. 7:22-24.

[33] St. Augustine (354-430), Bishop of Hippo; St. John Chrysostom (c. 347-407), Archbishop of Constantinople and Doctor; named Chrysostom, or "Golden Mouth" for his eloquent preaching;

....ous is to see that these holy men, notwithstanding their incessant labors, maintained themselves in constant union with God, for they quenched their thirst at the Source of life, drawing therefrom their vast capacity for work.

A great bishop, whose labors and cares were very numerous, being one day asked by a statesman who also was overburdened by the numerous duties of his office, the reason of his constant serenity and of the admirable results of his labors, replied, "To all your occupations, add every morning a half-hour's meditation, and your work will not only be expedited, but you will find time for even more work." And, in fact, did not St. Louis, King of France, find, in the eight or nine hours he daily devoted to the exercises of the interior life, the secret and the strength to apply himself with so great a solicitude to his official duties and the welfare of the people, that a certain socialist orator felt compelled to admit that not even in our times is so much done for the working classes as was done by St. Louis during his reign?

There is no selfishness in the interior life. As we have already seen, it is the pure and abundant source of the most generous charity for souls and for relieving human suffering. He who would call selfish and sterile the interior life of Mary and Joseph, because no exterior work of charity is attributed to them, would be absurd and, in some manner, even blasphemous. The very radiation on the world of an extensive interior life, the merits, prayers, and sacrifices applied to extend the benefits of the Redemption sufficed to constitute Mary as Queen of the Apostles and Joseph as patron of the universal Church. It is the interior life that imparts fecundity to apostolic works.

St. Vincent de Paul (1580-1660), founder of the Lazarist Fathers and the Sisters of Charity.

How much does he resemble Martha who, like her, complains of not being helped in his labors, because he considers merely his own work and its results. His lack of knowledge of the ways of God, although it may not go so far as to imagine that God cannot do without him, prevents him from appreciating the excellence of Mary's contemplation, for, like Martha, he says to Jesus, "Tell him to help me," and even exclaims, "for what is such a loss!" — reproaching as a waste of time the moments his more interior brethren in the apostolate devote to their intimate life with God.

"For them I sacrifice myself, *so that* they also may be sanctified in truth,"[34] replies the soul who grasps the meaning of "so that," and appreciates, therefore, the value of prayer and sacrifice, which add, as it were, to the Redeemer's tears and Blood, the tears of his own eyes and his heart's blood and help to draw down God's mercy on this sinful world. For the interior soul hears the horrible din of the crimes of mankind ascending heavenward and calling down on their perpetrators condign punishment, which it retards by the almighty power of its supplications, and thus it stays the hand of God about to hurl the shafts of divine justice on the criminals.

"Those who pray," said the great statesman Donoso Cortes, "do more for the world than those who combat; and if the world is growing worse, it is because there is now more fighting done than praying." "The hands raised heavenward," says Bossuet,[35] "overcome more enemies than those who strike." In their deserts, the ancient solitaries of the Thebaid were often animated with a zeal like that of St. Francis Xavier.[36] "They seemed," says St. Augustine, "to

[34] John 17:19.
[35] Jacques-Benigne Bossuet (1627-1704), Bishop of Meaux.
[36] St. Francis Xavier (1506-1552), Jesuit missionary to the East Indies.

have forsaken the world to a greater extent than it behooves them to do. But we do not consider that their prayers, having become more pure by their separation from the world, had also become more powerful and more necessary to the world."

A short, but fervent prayer, will usually promote a conversion more than will powerful arguments and elegant exhortations. He who prays treats with God Himself, the First Cause, and acts directly on the First Cause, the Source and Giver of grace; and without efficacious grace, no conversion is possible.

According to a revelation worthy of respect, ten thousand heretics were converted in consequence of a fervent prayer of St. Teresa;[37] for her ardent soul could not believe that a truly contemplative and interior soul can be indifferent to the infinite solicitude of Jesus Christ for the salvation of the souls whom He died to redeem and save! "I would be glad to remain in Purgatory until the day of judgment," she would say, "if I could thereby save one soul. Direct to this apostolic object," she would say to her nuns, "your prayers, your fasts, your penitential works, and your desires."

And, indeed, this is the very aim of the contemplative orders. They follow in spirit the travels and labors of apostolic men and nourish them, so to speak, with the superabundance of their prayers and austerities. Their prayers, after ascending heavenward, alight therefrom on the souls in the darkness of error and sin, bringing along to them supernatural light and strength.

No one here below can account for those distant conversions of pagans, or the heroic constancy of the persecuted Christians, or the heavenly joy of the martyred missionaries. All this is invisibly connected with the prayers of the cloistered religions. "They have,

---

[37] St. Teresa of Avila (1515-1582), Spanish Carmelite nun and mystic.

as it were, their fingers on the keyboard of the divine forgiveness," says a certain pious author, "and their silent and solitary souls preside over the salvation of souls and the conquests of the Church."

"I want Trappists in the Vicariate Apostolic," said Monsignor Favier of Peking. "I will not have them labor in the external ministry, so that they be not distracted from their life of prayer, penance, and their sacred studies, for I know the great assistance a fervent monastery of contemplatives is to our poor Chinese." At a later date, he said, "We have at last been able to penetrate into a region hitherto inaccessible, thanks to our dear Trappists."

"The prayers of ten Carmelite nuns will be of greater assistance than the preaching of twenty missionaries," wrote a bishop to the governor of Saigon.

The clergy, the religious of both sexes devoted to the active life and leading an interior life participate in the same power over the Heart of God, as we can see from the lives of Father Chevrier, St. John Bosco,[38] and many others. The Venerable Maria Taigi,[39] attending to her domestic duties, was a real apostle, and so were St. Benedict Joseph Labre,[40] Mr. Dupont, the "Holy Man of Tours,"[41] Colonel Taqueron, and many other laymen, filled with a similar ardor, were powerful in their works, because they were filled with the interior spirit. And General de Sonis, between two battles, would continue his apostolate through his union with God.

[38] St. John Bosco (1815-1888), priest who founded the Salesian Order.
[39] Bl. Maria Taigi (1769-1837), Italian widow and third-order Trinitarian, beatified in 1920.
[40] St. Benedict Joseph Labre (1748-1883), pilgrim and mendicant saint.
[41] St. Martin of Tours (c. 315-397), founder of a community of hermit monks and bishop.

Inner Strength for Active Apostles

The wonderfully successful apostolate of the Curé d'Ars was the result of his interior life, of his intimate union with God, for it enabled him to participate so abundantly in the divine power of converting souls. Were each diocese of our country to possess a Curé d'Ars, our country would be more effectively and thoroughly regenerated, than by all the resources, talent, learning, and activity of multitudes of apostles.

Notwithstanding our numerous schools; churches; learned, active, and eloquent clergy; able Catholic publications; Catholic institutions and works; and numerous converts every year, there is an unaccountable leakage, for the number of Catholics in the country is below what it ought to be, through divorces, mixed marriages, neglect of the religious education of children, and the absence of a Catholic atmosphere in the home life.

Chapter Three

The true apostolate calls for genuine zeal for souls

Someone may ask: Can we ever spend ourselves too much in our labors to save souls? Does not our great activity, our admirable devotedness fill every requirement? There is a saying that "he who labors for souls prays, and sacrifice comes before mental prayer." Does not Pope St. Gregory say that "there is nothing more pleasing to God than zeal for souls"?

But, in the first place, we should correctly explain St. Gregory's saying by the express teaching of St. Thomas. "To offer a spiritual sacrifice to God is to offer to Him something that gives Him glory. We cannot offer Him anything more pleasing than the salvation of a soul, but everyone should offer to God first his own soul according to Holy Scripture: 'Dost thou wish to please God? Have pity on thy own soul, pleasing God' [cf. Ecclus. 30:24; RSV = Sir. 30:23]. After accomplishing this sacrifice, we may procure a similar benefit to others. The more closely we, before all, unite ourselves to God, and afterward the soul of another, the more acceptable to Him is our sacrifice."

But this intimate, generous, and humble union of our soul to God can be effected only by means of mental prayer. To devote ourselves to or to cause others to lead a life of mental prayer is more pleasing to God than to devote ourselves or induce others to devote themselves to works of zeal. From this St. Thomas concludes that "St. Gregory does not intend to give the active life the preference over the contemplative, but means that to offer to God one soul is far more glorious and meritorious than any offering of earthly goods."[42]

But the necessity of the interior life should not, by any means, deter generous souls from works of zeal, if God's will, clearly known, demands this of them. Such a one should not give up such works or perform them carelessly, or desert them under the pretense of devoting all his efforts to his own sanctification and to attain a more perfect union with God. Such a one would be the victim of a pure illusion and would be liable to fall into great dangers of going astray. "Woe to me," says the great apostle St. Paul, "if I do not preach the gospel."[43]

With this reservation, we say that he who devotes himself to the conversion of souls and forgets the wants of his own soul falls into a still more dangerous illusion. God wills that we should love our neighbor as ourselves, but not *more than* ourselves; that is, our love for our neighbor should not induce us to neglect ourselves. In practice, we are bound to take greater care of our soul than of the souls of others, for our zeal must be regulated by charity, and we should, first of all, practice charity toward ourselves.

"I love Jesus Christ," says St. Alphonsus,[44] "and this is why I burn with the desire of giving Him souls — first my own soul, and

---

[42] *Summa Theologica*, II-II, Q. 182.

[43] Cf. 1 Cor. 9:16.

[44] St. Alphonsus Liguori (1696-1787), bishop, Doctor, writer, and founder of the Redemptorists.

then innumerable other souls." This is in accordance with the direction of St. Bernard: "Be thou everywhere thine own: he is unwise who is not his own."

The holy abbot Bernard of Clairvaux, who was a real phenomenon of apostolical zeal, is thus depicted by his secretary: "In the first place, Bernard was all to himself, and then all to all." The saint, among other things, wrote the following words to Pope Eugenius III:

> I do not mean that you should avoid treating of all secular matters. I merely exhort you not to devote yourself entirely thereto. If you are devoted to everybody, be also devoted to yourself. Otherwise what would it profit you to devote yourself to everyone, if you were to be lost? Reserve also some time, some care for yourself; if everyone comes to drink from your fountain, do not fail to drink yourself therefrom. Why should you alone suffer from thirst? Begin by first taking care of yourself. In vain would you devote yourself to the care of others, if you were to neglect your own self. Care for yourself first and last, and remember that, in all that concerns salvation, no one is nearer to you than your mother's son.

Let us now turn to Monsignor Dupanloup, the celebrated Bishop of Orleans; we quote the following passages from a note he wrote in one of his retreats:

> I have a terrible activity; it ruins my health, disturbs my piety, and is not necessary to my science — I must regulate this; God has given me the grace to discover that the great obstacle in me to leading an interior life is my own natural activity and the enticement of a multitude of occupations. I

own, moreover, that my lack of the interior life is the source of all my faults, troubles, spiritual dryness, disgust, and of my ill health. Wherefore I will direct all my efforts to the acquisition of the interior life which is wanting to me. And I have resolved, with God's grace, to keep the following resolutions:

1. I will always take more time than is needful for each thing, in order never to be in a hurry, or carried away by my anxiety for other things.

2. As I have always more things to do than time to do them properly, and therefore am preoccupied and carried away by my anxiety to perform them all, I will no longer consider so much what I have to do, as the time I can devote to business, and I will carefully spend that time, beginning with the most important matters, and I will not worry about those for which I have no time.

A jeweler prefers a very small diamond to several sapphires. In like manner, in accordance with the divinely established order, our intimacy with Him glorifies Him more than all the possible good we might procure to many souls to the detriment of our own spiritual progress. "Our heavenly Father," says one of the great masters of the spiritual life, Father Lallemant, S.J., "devotes more care to govern a soul, in which He reigns, than in governing all nature in the universe and in the civil government of all nations." He wills that our zeal for souls should not be greater than for our own spiritual progress. Sometimes He even allows a good work to disappear, if it becomes an obstacle to the development of charity (divine love) in the soul that is occupied with it."

Satan, on the contrary, does not hesitate to favor an apostolic man's superficial success, if, by doing so, he can prevent him

The true apostolate calls for genuine zeal

from making progress in the spiritual life, for his rage leads him to discover where the apostolic man's real treasures are in the sight of God. To suppress a diamond, Satan will easily grant a few sapphires.

Part Two

The active life
must be founded
on an interior life

Chapter Four

⁀

The interior life is
more excellent than the active

In the sight of God, the interior life is prior to and preferable to the active. In God is life, all life. He is Life itself. But it is not in His external activity, such as the Creation, that God manifests His life, His activity, most intensely, but in what theologians call His operations (activity) *ad intra* (within Himself), in that ineffable activity, the term of which is the perpetual generation of the Son and the incessant procession of the Holy Spirit. This is most especially His essential, eternal work (activity).

Let us consider the mortal life of our divine Savior, the perfect realization of the divine plan. It consisted of thirty years of recollection and solitude, then a retreat and penance of forty days, as a prelude to His short evangelical career; and how often in the course of His apostolic ministry did He not withdraw into a desert or a mountain to pray! "He withdrew into a desert and prayed" or "spent the night in prayer."[45] And here is something still more significant: Martha, giving Him hospitality in her house, was very busy preparing His meal; and her sister, Mary, instead of helping

---

[45] Cf. Luke 5:16; 6:12.

her, remained seated at the feet of Jesus, listening to His exhortations. Martha wished that Jesus would condemn what she called her sister's idleness, and bid her help her in her work, and thus proclaim the superiority of the active life over the contemplative; but Jesus replied, "Mary hath chosen the best part,"[46] and thereby declared the preeminence of the interior life over the active.

After our Savior's example, the Apostles, in the first place, reserved to themselves the office of prayer,[47] and then the ministry of the word (preaching), and turned the external occupations over to the deacons. In like manner, the popes, the holy Doctors, and the theologians declare that the interior life is in itself superior to the active.

Some years ago, when the atheistic government of France had passed iniquitous laws against the religious orders, a woman full of faith, and of remarkable virtue and courage, superioress-general of one of the most important teaching orders in France, was counseled by her ecclesiastical superiors to favor the secularization of her religions, or to give up the religious life as a means to continue the good works that would otherwise be completely ruined. In her perplexity as to the course she should follow, she at once secretly set out for Rome, obtained an audience with Pope Leo XIII, explained to him her doubt as to the course she should take, and the pressure exercised on her in favor of the apostolic works. The aged pope, after spending some moments in recollection and prayer, thus spoke to her:

> Before all, before the works, keep the religious life for those
> of your daughters who have the true spirit of their holy state

---

[46] Luke 10:42.
[47] Acts 6:4.

and love a life of prayer. And if you cannot preserve both the life of prayer and these works, God will, if necessary, raise up in France others to perform these works. As for you and your Sisters, you will, by your interior life and especially by your prayers and sacrifices, prove more useful to France by remaining true religious, even out of France, than by remaining on its soil deprived of the treasures of your consecration to God.

In a letter addressed to a great institute exclusively engaged in teaching, Pope Pius X gave expression to his views:

We learn that an opinion is beginning to spread according to which you should give the first place to the education of children, and give then only the second place to the religious profession, under the plea that such is the want of our times. We absolutely do not wish that such an opinion should be held by anyone among you, or in other religious institutes devoted to education. Wherefore, all of you should firmly hold that the religious life is far above the ordinary Christian life, and that if you have the grave obligation toward your neighbor to engage in teaching, your obligations binding you to God (as religious) are far more grave.

In fact, the very existence and the principal object of the religious life is the acquisition of the interior life. "The contemplative life," says St. Thomas, "is more excellent than the active life and is preferable to it." According to St. Bonaventure, the contemplative life is "more sublime, more secure, richer in merits, more sweet and stable than the active life." It is more sublime, for the active is occupied with men, but the contemplative leads us into the domains of the highest truths, without turning us away or withdrawing us from the very Principle of all life. It seeks God, the Principle of all being; its horizon is more sublime, its field of action much more vast. "Martha," says Richard of St. Victor,[48] "performed manual work in one place only; but Mary, by her charity, labors in many places and in many works, extends her usefulness to all things, and embraces all things; and Martha, compared with Mary, does but little."

• *The contemplative life is more secure,* for in it there are fewer dangers. In the life that is principally active, the soul is agitated, feverish, and scatters its energy and is thereby weakened. It labors under a threefold disadvantage of being anxious in its thoughts, disturbed in its affections and by a multitude of occupations; hence, its efforts and acts are divided. But in the interior life, there is but one thing, union with God, and that is the only thing necessary; all the rest is only accessory and is accomplished by virtue of this union and fortified by it.

• *It is a life richer in merits.* "With contemplation come all goods."[49] "It is the best part."[50] In it, greater merits abound; it increases the energy of the will and the degree of sanctifying grace, and causes the soul to act through divine love (love of God).

• *It is a sweeter life.* The truly interior soul surrenders himself to God's holy pleasure, accepts with equanimity both what is pleasant and what is unpleasant, rejoices in affliction, and feels happy in carrying the cross, for Christ's yoke is sweet and His burden light.[51]

[48] Richard of St. Victor (d. 1173), Scottish mystical theologian.
[49] Cf. Wisd. 7:11.
[50] Luke 10:42.
[51] Matt. 11:30.

• *It is a more stable life.* However intense it may be, the active life has its limits on earth. Preaching, teaching, works of every kind: all this ceases at the threshold of eternity. The interior life alone has no decline: "It shall not be taken away from her."[52] By it, our sojourn on earth is but a continuous ascension toward light, which death renders incomparably more bright and rapid. Hence, St. Bernard says, "In it, a man lives more purely, falls more rarely, rises more promptly, walks more securely, receives grace more abundantly, dies more confidently, is purified more quickly, and is rewarded more plentifully."

---

[52] Luke 10:42.

Chapter Five

Nourishing your own soul enables you to nourish the souls of others

"Be ye perfect as your heavenly Father is perfect."[53] With due proportion, the divine mode of action should be the rule or criterion of our interior and exterior life.

To give is a property pertaining to the divine nature. Experience shows us that God is profuse in His gifts to all beings, and more especially to man; and since the creation, the whole universe is the recipient of His inexhaustible beneficence.

God grants to man far more than merely external benefits, for He has given him His only-begotten Son, equal to Himself. Jesus came from Heaven to enrich us with His graces through the sacraments, and especially through the Blessed Eucharist. He pours His benefits upon us without measure or stint, for "We have all received from His fullness."[54] We should, therefore, be apostolic men assuming the noble task of sanctifying others. According to St. Bernard, our word is the consideration or interior spirit formed in us by divine grace. This spirit should vivify all the manifestations

[53] Matt. 5:48.
[54] Cf. John 1:16.

of our zeal, but when we dispense it incessantly for the benefit of our neighbor, we should also incessantly renew it by the means Jesus offers us.

The soul of an apostle should be ours, but, in the first place, it should be inundated with light and inflamed by love, so that, when reflecting light and warmth, it may also enlighten and enkindle other souls. What they have seen and what they have "considered with their eyes and almost touched with their hands"[55] they shall teach to men.

From the foregoing we may deduce this conclusion: "The active life should proceed from the contemplative, and should transfer it and continue it externally, and cling to it as much as possible." This is the teaching of the Fathers and Doctors of the Church. "Before allowing our tongue to speak," says St. Augustine, "we should raise our thirsting soul to God, that we may then pour out that with which we have been filled."

In the "Celestial Hierarchy," we read, "We must first receive what we are to impart, for the Creator has laid down this rule in things divine: he whose mission is to distribute them must first participate himself in them and be abundantly filled with the graces which God wishes to grant to souls through his ministry. Then, and then only, shall he be permitted to enable others to share therein."

"If you are wise," says St. Bernard, "you will not be a mere supply pipe, but a reservoir. The former lets the water flow through without retaining any itself, whilst the latter, after being itself full, and without losing a drop, pours out its superabundance to fertilize the fields. How many in the Church who are devoted to apostolic works, like mere supply pipes, remain dry, whilst endeavoring to impart fertility to others."

---

[55] Cf. 1 John 1:1.

A cause is superior to its effect. Wherefore he who is to perfect others should possess greater perfection, if he wishes to succeed. As a mother is able to nourish her baby only in proportion as she nourishes herself, so in like manner, confessors, spiritual directors, preachers, catechists, and teachers must first assimilate that with which they are afterward to nourish the children of the Church. Truth and divine love are the elements to be imparted to the latter. The interior life is indispensable for so imparting divine truth and charity, as to render them a life-giving nourishment.

Chapter Six

⁀

The fruitful union of the contemplative and active lives

The base, the end, and the means of an apostolic work must be rendered fruitful by the interior life. We do not speak here of certain works organized under some pious exterior form, the real object of which is to procure for their founders public applause and a certain notoriety, and for the success of which even most unjustifiable means are adopted. There are other works, whose object and means are irreproachable, but their originators, for want of firm faith in the power of the supernatural life, obtain but poor results in spite of their great efforts and ability.

To understand precisely what an apostolic work ought to be, the author, intending to establish such a work for young men, first visited similar institutions; one, at Marseilles, was under the direction of two holy priests, the Abbe Allemant and Canon Timon David. The latter, after speaking of the usual Catholic young men's clubs or societies, and their amusements and similar means of benefitting members and attaching them to their Faith, spoke as follows:

> In the beginning, I also considered these means to be indispensable, but the further we proceed, the more my object

and my means become supernatural, for I see clearly that every apostolic work built on a human foundation is destined to perish, and that Providence blesses only those works which aim at bringing men to God by the interior life. The musical instruments, theatricals, gymnastics have long ago been laid aside, and yet our work is far more prosperous than ever before, for we now have a better understanding of the whole matter. Our ideal should not consist merely in affording our young men the choice of lawful amusements and distractions, in order to keep them from forbidden company and pleasures, and to give them only a coating of Christianity by requiring of them a mechanical assistance at Mass on Sundays and the fulfillment of their Easter duties. But we should heed the Lord's command: "Launch out into the deep" (Luke 5:4). We should start with the noble ambition to obtain, at every casting of our net, that a certain number of young men should energetically resolve to lead a truly fervent Christian life; that is, make meditation every morning, hear Mass daily, if possible, do spiritual reading, and make frequent and fervent holy Communions.

As for us, we should strive to impart to that small chosen flock an ardent love for Jesus Christ, the spirit of prayer, of self-denial and watchfulness over themselves. Develop carefully among them a hunger for the holy Eucharist. Then gradually inspire them with zeal toward other young men, in order to make of them apostles, good, openhearted, devoted, ardent and manly, tactful and sincere. Before two years are over, you will be able to tell me whether amusements and games are really necessary to ensure success with young men. As to the married men of mature age, you should strengthen their faith by simple, but well-prepared series of familiar conferences or lectures in the long winter evenings, not only to answer victoriously the objections and erroneous principles of their fellow workmen, but also to resist and overcome the more perfidious influence of certain newspapers and other publications. Impart to the men firm and unshaken convictions that will enable them to overcome all human respect and practice their Faith without faltering, and you will soon witness very appreciable results. But you must continue your labors until the men are endowed with a piety, real, ardent, fervent, convinced, and enlightened.

Do not aim at great numbers, but be very careful in your choice, especially in the beginning. The first members should become a nucleus of lay apostles, of whom Jesus, Mary, and Joseph should be the center, and yourself the instrument. In the beginning especially, your place of meeting should be simple and humble, without costly ornamentation or furniture to attract public attention. Publicity will not bring success. But above all, you must contribute *yourself*, your efforts, your labors, your devotedness, not in preparing and organizing plays and the like, but by accumulating in yourself the life of prayer, for only in proportion as you yourself live by the love of God will you be able to kindle it in the hearts of others.

Labor and success in the apostolate are all based on the interior life. How great would be the good produced in a city by a Catholic association leading a truly supernatural life! It would prove a powerful leaven of sanctification, and the angels alone could tell how fertile it would be in fruits of salvation and sanctity. If all who are devoted to apostolic works knew the power of the lever they hold and would use as a fulcrum the Heart of Jesus and a life in union with His divine Heart, they would again raise up our France [the speaker's country] in spite of the efforts and laws of Satan's minions!

⤿

The interior life and the active life
mutually require one another

"Just as the love of God," says St. Isidore,[56] "reveals itself by acts of the interior life, so also the love of the neighbor manifests itself by the operations of the exterior life; and as the love of God and the love of the neighbor are practically inseparable, it follows that these two forms of life cannot subsist without each other." This is also the teaching of Suarez[57] and St. Thomas. "Those who are called to the works of the active life," says the latter, "would be mistaken, were they to imagine that they are thereby dispensed from the acts of the contemplative life, for they should be added to the duties of the active life. Hence, these two modes of life, far from excluding one another, require, presuppose, mingle with, and complete each other; and if one of them should have the larger share, it should be the contemplative, which is the more perfect and the more necessary of the two."

Action, to prove fertile, stands in need of contemplation; and when the latter has reached a certain degree of intensity, it pours out on the former some of its superabundance and enables the soul to draw directly from the Heart of God the graces that the active life is charged with distributing. This explains why, in a saint,

---

[56] St. Isidore of Seville (d. 636), bishop, writer, and Doctor who converted the Visigoths from the Arian heresy.

[57] Francisco Suarez (1548-1617), Jesuit theologian.

action and contemplation united together in perfect harmony impart perfect unity to his life. For instance, St. Bernard was at the same time the most contemplative and the most active person of his time. In him, contemplation and action so perfectly harmonized together, that he, at one and the same time, appeared wholly devoted to external works and all absorbed in the presence and the love of God.

Father St. Jure, S.J., commenting on Canticles 8:6 — "Place me as a seal upon thy heart and as a seal upon thy arm" — says that "the heart signifies the interior, contemplative life, and the arm, the exterior, active life, and that Holy Scripture mentions the heart and the arm together in order to show that both modes of life can be found perfect together in one person. The heart is mentioned first, because it is far more noble and necessary than the arm. Moreover, contemplation is likewise far more excellent and perfect and more meritorious than action. The heart beats day and night; were it to cease for a moment, death would ensue. The arm is only an integral part of the body and moves at intervals. Hence, we should sometimes cease performing external works, but should never relax from our application to spiritual things."

The heart imparts life and strength to the arm by means of the blood it sends to it; otherwise the arm would wither away. In like manner, the contemplative life, the life of union with God, through the light and perpetual assistance that the soul receives from this intimacy, vivifies the exterior occupations and is alone capable of imparting to them a supernatural character and real usefulness. Without the contemplative life, all languishes; all is sterile and full of imperfections.

Man, alas, too often separates what God has united; hence, perfect union between the contemplative and the active life is seldom found. Moreover, it cannot be realized without a series of precautions, which are too often neglected, such as: never to undertake what is beyond one's strength; to see habitually but simply in all things the will of God; never to engage oneself in apostolic works, unless God wills it, and then only as much as pleases Him and with the sole desire of practicing charity; from the very start, to offer to Him one's labors and, in laboring, frequently to renew one's resolution of acting for Him and by Him, by means of holy thoughts and aspirations; in all labors, however absorbing they may be, always to keep oneself peaceful and self-possessed; and to leave success solely to God and keep free from all anxiety, in order to be alone with Jesus Christ. These are the wise counsels the masters of the spiritual life indicate as means of being united to Jesus Christ.

Sometimes our occupations may become so numerous as to prevent us from enjoying union with Jesus, but this of itself will not injure us. If this state is prolonged, we should bear it, grieve over it, and dread above all to get used to it. We are naturally weak and inconstant. When our spiritual life is neglected, we soon lose all relish for it. When we are absorbed by material tasks, we are apt soon to take delight therein. On the other hand, if we sincerely regret our inability to devote ourselves to the practices of the interior life, in order to devote so much more time to God's works, and yet strive as much as we can not to lose sight of God, our disposition will prevent our numerous occupations from doing us any injury, and God will, as it were, work with us and support us.

*The true apostolate is a union
of the contemplative and the active lives*

The union of the contemplative and the active lives constitutes the true apostolate, the principal work of the Christian religion,

The fruitful union of the contemplative and active lives

according to St. Thomas. The apostolate supposes souls capable of ardent zeal for and devotedness to the supernatural order.

"The apostolate of the man of prayer," says St. Bonaventure, "is the conquering word endowed with a divine mission and zeal for souls and fruitful in conversions." The apostolate of the saint is the sowing of the seed of faith, the word of God, says Pope St. Leo.[58] It is the fiery love of God, enkindled on Pentecost by the Holy Spirit in the hearts of the Apostles, to enable them to propagate it among all nations. It is the same fire that our divine Savior had come to cast upon the earth.[59] The sublimity of this ministry consists in laboring and providing for the salvation of others, without loss or injury to the apostle. To transmit to men's minds divine truth is, in fact, a ministry worthy of the very angels. To contemplate truth is good indeed. To impart it to others is better still. Reflecting light is more than merely receiving it. To give light is better than to shine under a bushel. The soul is nourished by contemplation, but, by the apostolate, it gives itself.

This mingling of the apostolate and all the outpouring of its zeal with contemplation and its sublime elevations to God has produced the greatest saints, such as Sts. Dionysius, Martin, Bernard, Dominic,[60] Francis of Assisi,[61] Francis Xavier, Philip Neri,[62] Francis de Sales,[63] and Alphonsus. They were ardent contemplatives as well as apostles.

---

[58] St. Leo the Great (d. 461), Pope from 440 and Doctor.

[59] Luke 12:49.

[60] St. Dominic (c. 1170-1221), founder of the Dominican Order.

[61] St. Francis of Assisi (1182-1226), founder of the Franciscan Order.

[62] St. Philip Neri (1515-1595), founder of the Congregation of the Oratory.

[63] St. Francis de Sales (1567-1622), Bishop of Geneva.

Inner Strength for Active Apostles

Interior life and active life! Holiness in apostolic works! What a powerful and fertile union! What prodigies are wrought by such a union!

O God,
deign to give Thy Church
many such apostolic men,
but at the same time,
deign to revive in their hearts
a longing to "spend themselves
and be spent" for the salvation
of their fellowmen
and an ardent thirst
for a life of prayer.
Impart to Thine apostle
a contemplative activity
and an active contemplation,
and they will gain the victories
which Thou didst promise them
before ascending to Heaven.

Part Three

Growing holy
through apostolic works

Chapter Seven

∼

Apostolic works offer
means of holiness to the apostle

Our divine Savior expressly requires that those He associates with
Himself in His apostolate should make progress in virtue. This is
evident in almost every page of St. Paul's letters to Timothy and to
Titus and in our Savior's messages to the bishops of Asia Minor in
the second and third chapters of the book of Revelation.

The apostle who is called by God, should have an absolute
confidence in God's justice and goodness, that he will receive
from Him all the graces he needs to sanctify himself, and that he
will be able to sanctify himself, provided that he, on his part, faithfully corresponds with these graces.

The learned Alvarez de Paz[64] says:

He who devotes himself to works of charity should not
imagine that they will prevent him from observing the
practices of the interior life. He should, on the contrary, be
convinced that these works dispose him admirably to lead
an interior life. Not only reason itself and the teaching of

---

[64] Alvarez de Paz (1560-1620), Spanish mystic.

the Fathers tell us this, but even daily experience confirms it. We see persons devoted to works of zeal, of charity, such as preaching, hearing confessions, visiting and caring for the sick, religious teachers, and so forth, leading a truly holy life, an interior life.

The sacrifices exacted by the apostolic works draw from the glory of God and the sanctification of souls so great a supernatural virtue, and so great a fertility of merits, that the apostle, if he only wills, can daily rise a whole degree in charity and union with God, that is, in holiness.

But where, in certain cases, the apostolic labors would be to the laborer a grave and proximate occasion of grievous sin against faith or purity, on account of his frailty, the will of God is that he should give up such apostolic works. These, however, are exceptional cases. In all other cases, experience proves that, through the interior life, God provides His laborers with all the means necessary for overcoming all temptations and dangers, and for making progress in virtue and holiness.

⌒

Holiness manifests itself in acts of charity

Let us now see in what this progress consists. A paradoxical word of the judicious and witty St. Teresa will enable us to precise our thought. "Since I am prioress, charged with many works and obliged to travel often, I commit many more faults. And nevertheless, as I combat generously and spend myself only for God, I feel that I draw nearer and nearer to Him." Her weakness was indeed more manifest then than when she was in the rest and silence of the cloister, but she does not worry over it, for the supernatural generosity of her devotedness and her efforts in the spiritual combat, now more accentuated than before, furnished her occasions of victories that more than counterbalanced the surprises of a frailty that previously existed in a more latent state. "Our union with God," says St. John of the Cross,[65] "resides in the union of our will with His, and is measured by it alone." Instead of seeing, through a false idea of spirituality, the possibility of making progress in union with God only in quiet and solitude, St. Teresa maintains, on the contrary, that an exterior activity truly imposed by God, and exercised in the conditions He requires, that is, conditions which nourish the spirit of sacrifice, humility, self-denial, and ardor for and devotedness to the reign of God, actually increases the intimate union of one's soul with God, and brings one nearer and nearer to holiness.

Holiness, in fact, resides, before all, in charity, and an apostolic work worthy of the name is "charity in act," or actual charity, for, says St. Gregory, "the proof of our love is the showing of our work." Love is proved by works of self-devotedness, which God requires of His laborers as a proof of devotedness to Him. "Feed my lambs; feed my sheep,"[66] was the form of love Jesus demanded of St. Peter, as a proof of the sincerity of his protestations of love. St. Francis of Assisi would not consider himself a friend of Jesus Christ if he did not devote himself to the salvation of the souls redeemed by Jesus Christ. Moreover, our divine Judge, by saying at the last day to those who had in life practiced the works of mercy toward their neighbor, "As long as you did it to the least of my brethren, you did it to me,"[67] shows that he considers that they

---

[65] St. John of the Cross (1542-1591), Spanish Carmelite mystic, and reformer of the Carmelite Order.

[66] John 21:15, 17.

[67] Cf. Matt. 25:40.

who are engaged in the works of mercy are animated by the same charity that animates the contemplative in his austerities, combats, and prayers.

The active life is employed in works of devotedness. It proceeds through the paths of sacrifice, following Jesus as workman, shepherd, missionary, and miracle-worker, universal physician and loving and indefatigable provider of all the wants of the needy. The active life is mindful of and lives by this saying of our divine Master: "I am in the midst of you as he that serveth."[68] "The Son of man did not come to be served, but to serve."[69] It travels along the road of human miseries, pronouncing the word that enlightens, sowing all around an abundance of graces and benefits.

Thanks to the insight of its faith, to the intuition of its love, it discovers in the most wretched, in the meanest of sufferers, Jesus Christ Himself, naked, mournful, despised by all, the great leper, the mysterious condemned one, pursued by the eternal justice, struck by God and afflicted, the Man of Sorrows, covered with wounds and blood, deformed and crushed like a worm trodden upon. "We have seen Him," says the prophet, "and there was no sightliness . . . despised and the most abject of men, a man of sorrows . . . and His look was as if it were hidden, and we esteemed Him not."[70] But the active life recognizes Him well, and on its knees, with eyes filled with tears, it beholds Him in the poor, the needy, the suffering, and even in the outcast.

The active life ameliorates mankind and imparts fertility to the world through its acts of generosity, its labors and fatigues; it sows Heaven with its merits. It is a holy life rewarded by God, for He

---

[68] Luke 22:27.

[69] Matt. 20:28.

[70] Isa. 53:2-3.

confers Heaven as well on him who gives drink to the thirsty, as on the learned who has written good books, and on the great labors of the apostle, and will canonize on the last day, before Heaven and earth, all who have been devoted to works of mercy and charity.

❧

Apostolic works can pose dangers to salvation

A sad experience of our ministry discloses to us that the works which should be means of progress to the laborers become, to some, occasions of spiritual ruin; some of them acknowledge it, saying, "It is my overeagerness that has brought on my fall! My excessive devotion to and love for the active life filled me with great joy at my success, and this, together with the deceits of Satan, has led me to be so absorbed in laboring for others, as to neglect my own spiritual wants, prayer and meditation; and then, when temptation came, I yielded in the weakness caused by my lack of spiritual nourishment."

"I am smitten, as grass, because I forgot to eat my bread."[71] "Such a one," says St. Augustine, "labored hard and went very fast, but out of the right road," and thus he went astray. His apparent success blinded him, making him proud, forgetful of God and of his soul's wants; and the result was fatal to him. It was against such a misfortune that St. Bernard warned Pope Eugenius III: "I fear," wrote the saint to him, "that, in the midst of your numerous occupations, you, despairing of getting through with them, might harden your soul. You should be more prudent and lay aside these occupations, at least for a time, lest they dominate over you, and infallibly lead you whither you do not wish, that is, to obduracy of heart, for to this will those occupations of yours lead, if you

---

[71] Ps. 101:5 (RSV = Ps. 102:4).

continue to devote yourself entirely to them, without setting apart sufficient time for your own soul."

What is more holy, more august than to govern the Church of God? Is there anything more useful to the glory of God and the welfare of souls? And nevertheless, St. Bernard calls them "accursed occupations," if they become an obstacle to the interior life of him whom God has called to perform them. This frightens us and causes us to reflect, and we would protest, had this not been written by St. Bernard, a holy Doctor of the Church.

⌢

The active man who lacks the interior life becomes worldly

The active man who lacks the interior life may not yet be tepid, but he will surely become so. His tepidity will not be a tepidity of frailty or feeling, but a willful tepidity. Such a tepidity is, in effect, a peace with deliberate venial sin. Such a peace deprives the soul of the security of salvation, for it disposes and even leads the soul to mortal sin, according to the teaching of St. Alphonsus. Cardinal Lavigerie wrote as follows to his missionaries: "You should be firmly persuaded that, for an apostle, there is no medium; he must be really holy, at least in desire and in faithful and courageous efforts; or he will be gradually perverted."

Let us first advert to the germ of corruption, which concupiscence keeps up in our nature, the relentless war waged against us by our exterior and interior enemies and the dangers threatening us on every side. Then let us endeavor to represent to ourselves what happens to him who devotes himself to the apostolate without being sufficiently forearmed against its dangers.

For instance, N. feels an interior desire to consecrate himself to the works of the apostolate. He lacks experience, but possesses a certain amount of ardor, is fond of the work and ready to labor for success. His conduct is good; he is pious, but more through feeling or habit than as a result of firm resolution to seek only to please God. As yet, he possesses but little of the true interior life. He has many good qualities and is sincerely desirous to be faithful to God. Soon after his entrance into the active life, there arise in his path many distracting circumstances and allurements, from which he had hitherto been safeguarded by the atmosphere and influence surrounding his pious home, seminary, community, novitiate, or a wise guide. But now an increasing dissipation of mind, a natural curiosity to know all, or presumption, sensuality, jealousy, or some other natural disposition will entangle him in a relentless warfare for which he is ill-prepared and in which he frequently receives spiritual wounds. And does he, who is only superficially pious, even think of resisting, when he is absorbed in the too-natural satisfaction that he feels devoting all his activity and talents to the excellent cause in which he is engaged? And instead of striving to overcome this natural satisfaction, he does all he can to excite it the more. Satan, moreover, is on the watch to capture what he considers an excellent prey.

At last a day comes when this laborer has a glimpse of his danger. His angel guardian has spoken, and his conscience reproaches him. He would need to recover his self-possession, thoroughly examine himself in the calm of a retreat, and firmly resolve to bind himself irrevocably to a strict rule of life, even if his dearly loved occupation had to suffer therefrom for a time. Alas! this is rather late for him to do this, for he has already enjoyed the satisfaction of some success in his work and defers remedying his dangerous state to some later date, saying, "Today, this week, this month, I have no time. I must first finish the work I have now in hand." And he feels happy in finding pretexts to defer the necessary remedy, for the very idea of facing his own conscience is unbearable. Now is the moment when Satan can labor at his ease to effect his ruin, for the soil is prepared. Action has now become a passion for his intended victim; therefore Satan works this passion into a fever! To recollect himself and lay aside his labors for a time had appeared insupportable to him; hence, the Devil inspires him with a horror of it and suggests to him fresh projects for the glory of God and the salvation of souls!

And now that man, hitherto good and devoted, is, through weakness, more and more accentuated, about to tread a slippery path that is apt to cause his fall. Feeling disturbed by a vague consciousness that all his agitation is not in accord with the Heart of God, he plunges more deeply than ever into the active life in order to find rest. His faults accumulate. What formerly worried his upright conscience is now considered a mere scruple. He claims that we must now be up-to-date in our labors, lay aside all antiquated ways and means, make ourselves popular, and progress with the times. Gradually he becomes worldly-minded and finally falls!

Let us examine how this happened to him.

Selfish motives in the apostolate lead to tepidity
In the first place, such a one gradually lost the clearness and power of his convictions in reference to the supernatural life, the supernatural world, and the economy of our Savior's plan and action concerning the interior life and the relation of the apostle and his activity. He now sees the works to which he devotes himself only through a deceitful mirage. His vanity has become the pedestal of his pretended good intention. "What will you have?" replied a puffed-up preacher to his flatterers. "God has given me the gift of speech, and I am thankful to Him for it." Such an

apostle seeks himself rather than God. Reputation, glory, and personal interests are number one with him. To him the saying of St. Paul, "Were I to please men, I would not be a servant of Christ,"[72] is devoid of sense. The want of a supernatural base is either caused or followed by dissipation of mind, forgetfulness of the divine presence, the giving up of the practice of spontaneous prayers and of the custody of the heart, and the lack of a tender conscience and regularity of life. Tepidity is near, if it has not already gained the mastery.

In the second place, the supernatural man, being wholly devoted to duty, is a miser of his time and therefore employs it in accordance with a fixed rule. He is convinced that otherwise his active life would soon become a mere natural life and lead him into a life of ease and comfort, of mere feeling from morning until night. The active worker who lacks a supernatural base will soon experience this. The want of the spirit of faith in the use of his time will soon lead him to give up spiritual reading. If, however, he still reads, he no longer studies, and unless prompted by vanity, he prefers to improvise in his preaching and feels confident of being admirably successful in so doing. He prefers magazines to useful books. He follows no order in his reading, but acts like a butterfly fluttering from flower to flower. The law of work, which is a means of preservation from sin and of penance, he disregards by wasting his leisure hours and seeking too many distractions. And as he has not enough time for attending to all his tasks and social duties and his supposed necessary relaxation or recreation, he listens willingly to Satan suggesting, "You need not devote so much time to prayer and meditation and the like." Consequently, he first shortens his meditations and other pious practices, and then sometimes

[72] Cf. Gal. 1:10.

omits them, pretexting the want of time. Now, as he becomes careless and no longer seriously examines his conscience, he does not see his numerous venial sins, nor endeavor to correct them, and practically gives up mental prayer and his rule of life, and thus reaches the stage of tepidity.

His next step is carelessness in reciting the Divine Office. This prayer of the Church, and really his official prayer, should fill him with joy and impart to him the strength to lead a holy life and sanctify his fellowmen. The liturgical life, a source of light, joy, strength, merits, and graces, has become for him a disagreeable task that he performs carelessly and mechanically, merely to get rid of it. The personal and obscure, but hearty sacrifice of praise, supplication, thanksgiving, and reparation is now meaningless to him. Formerly he would be filled with joy when reciting the psalms, reflecting interiorly: "I will sing praises to Thee, O God, in sight of the angels."[73] Now his excessive solicitude for his labors and his habitual dissipation of mind keep him from paying attention to the meaning of the words he recites, from deriving benefit therefrom, and lead him to precipitation, to unjustified interruptions, to put off the recitation of his office to the last moment, and instead of enriching him in grace and merits, the "sacrifice of praise" becomes for him like a litany of sins!

Finally, since, in the life of the apostles, all things are connected together, the sacraments now are administered or received by him merely as something worthy of respect, indeed, but they are no longer felt as something really divine and imparting divine grace. The presence of Jesus in the tabernacle or in the sacred tribunal of Penance, and even the Holy Sacrifice of the Mass no longer fill him with an awe mingled with childlike confidence, and

---

[73] Ps. 137:1 (RSV = Ps. 138:1).

their fruits are no longer so apparent or comforting and strengthening, his heart remains mostly cold and unmoved, and his will grows weak.

The previously quoted Father Lallement, speaking of the few who go astray, says, "Certain apostolical men never labor purely for God; they seek themselves in all things and always secretly have in view their own interests together with the glory of God even in their holiest undertakings. They spend their life in mingling nature with grace; and it is only when death is at hand that they realize their illusion and dread appearing before the tribunal of the divine Judge."

Although the celebrated missionary and orator Father Combalot was not an apostolic man of the class just alluded to, he nevertheless dreaded judgment, like so many apostles before him. The priest, after administering the last sacraments, said to him, "Yours has been the life of a worthy priest. Your thousands of sermons will plead with God in your behalf, for the insufficiency of the interior life, which you are deploring." Combalot replied, "My sermons! In what a different light do I now see them! If our Lord does not first mention them to me, I will be careful not to say a word about them!" By the light of eternity dawning upon him, that venerated priest beheld in his best works of zeal alarming imperfections that he attributed to his lack of a sufficiently interior life!

Cardinal du Perron, the celebrated theologian and controversialist, testified, when about to die, his regret at having been more careful to improve his mind by the study of the sciences, than by the exercises of the interior life.

Chapter Eight

The interior life is the base of the holiness of the apostle

Because holiness is the interior life in very close union with the will of God, the soul, unless through a miracle of grace, does not usually reach such a state until, by dint of numerous and arduous efforts, it has passed through all the stages of the purgative and illuminative lives.[74] It is a law of the spiritual life that, in the course of sanctification, the action of God and the action of the soul proceed inversely. The action of God increases daily, and the soul becomes daily less and less active. God's action in the perfect differs from His action in beginners. In the latter, it is less apparent, for it induces and upholds their watchfulness and supplications, and thereby offers them the means of obtaining grace for renewed efforts. In the perfect, God's action is more complete, sometimes requiring from them only a simple consent to unite

---

[74] The purgative and illuminative lives are two developmental stages of the interior life. The purgative stage, that of souls at the beginning of their spiritual journey, is the one in which the soul strives to overcome its passions. Those who have reached the illuminative stage have control of their passions and are more and more enlightened about the spiritual life.

their soul to His supreme action. The beginners, and even the tepid and the sinners, whom God wishes to draw nearer to Himself at first feel drawn to seek God, and then to prove to Him more and more their desire to please Him, and finally to rejoice in all the providential occasions afforded them to overcome their self-love and establish in themselves the reign of Jesus only. In these cases, the divine action is limited to incentives.

In the saint, the divine action is more powerful, more complete. The saint, in the midst of fatigue and suffering, oppressed by humiliations, or crushed by disease, has only to surrender himself to the divine action, for otherwise he would be unable to bear the agonies that, in God's design, are to finish ripening him for Heaven. In him, these words of St. Paul are realized: "God subjects all things to Himself, that God may be all in all things."[75] The saint lives so much by Jesus that he seems no longer to live by his own life, for he can say with St. Paul: "I live, now not I, but Christ liveth in me."[76] In him, the spirit of Jesus thinks, decides, and acts. Undoubtedly the deification in him is still very far from reaching the intensity it will have when he will be in glory, and yet his state reflects already the characteristics of the beatific union.

The beginners, the tepid, and even the simply fervent are very far from reaching this state. The beginner, like an apprentice in a trade, will find sanctification very hard work indeed. His progress will be slow, nor will his work be noticeable. The fervent will find less difficulty and make quicker progress.

But the intentions of Divine Providence concerning every class of apostolic men are invariable. God wills that every kind of apostolic works should be means of sanctification to the laborers

---

[75] Cf. 1 Cor. 15:28.
[76] Gal. 2:20.

called thereto. The apostolate is not dangerous to him who is already holy, nor does it exhaust his spiritual strength, but furnishes him with many occasions of increasing in virtue and merits. The apostolate, on the other hand, is apt to cause spiritual anemia in those who are but feebly united to God, in whom the love of prayer, the spirit of sacrifice, and the habit of custody of the heart are only weakly developed.

God never refuses this habit to earnest prayer and reiterated proofs of fidelity. He pours it out liberally into generous souls who have gradually transformed their faculties and rendered them supple to divine inspirations, and capable of cheerfully accepting contradictions, failure, losses, and deceptions.

The interior life forearms the apostolic man
against the dangers of the active ministry

"It is difficult," says St. Thomas, "to care for souls on account of its dangers." The apostle who lacks the interior spirit knows not the dangers he is in and is like one unarmed traveling in places infested with brigands. But the true apostle dreads them and daily takes the necessary precautions against them, for he makes a serious examination of his conscience to discover wherein he is especially vulnerable. Were this the only advantage of the interior life, it would already powerfully contribute to preserving him from being surprised on his way, for a danger foreseen is already half-overcome. But its usefulness is far from ending here.

It becomes a complete armor for the apostolic workman, for St. Paul says, "Take unto you the helmet of salvation, that you may be able to stand against the deceits of the Devil . . . and may be able to resist the evil day, and to stand in all things perfect [that is, sanctify all you do]. . . . Have your loins girt about with truth [that is, let your intention be pure, concentrating in God your thoughts, desires, and affections, and avoid going astray by seeking ease, pleasure, and distractions]; having on the breastplate of justice [that is, of charity, which imparts a manly heart, a sure protection against the seduction of creatures, the spirit of the world, and the assaults of Satan]; your feet shod with the preparation of the gospel of peace [the interior life teaches him to proceed with discretion, modesty, and restraint, combining the simplicity of the dove with the prudence of the serpent]; in all things taking the shield of faith, wherewith you may be able to extinguish all the fiery darts of the wicked one [Satan and the world will endeavor to lead you astray by false doctrines and enervate you by unsound maxims; the interior life will protect you by faith, or the true knowledge of your nothingness and helplessness without divine grace, and the necessity of earnest prayer and a confidence impervious to the assaults of pride]; and take unto you the helmet of salvation and the sword of the Spirit."[77]

Thus armed, the apostolic man may labor without fear, for his zeal, enkindled by meditating on the gospel, fortified by the Eucharist, has the sword wherewith to conquer his enemies and gain many souls to Jesus Christ.

⌒

The interior life
reinvigorates the apostolic man

In the midst of the turmoil of affairs, and notwithstanding his habitual combat with the world, the saint alone knows how to safeguard his interior spirit and to direct all his thoughts and intentions to God alone. In him, all his external activity is so

[77] Cf. Eph. 6:11, 13-17.

supernaturalized and burning with charity, that far from diminishing his strength, it necessarily brings him an increase of grace. In others, even in the fervent, a longer or shorter time devoted to the apostolate causes this supernatural life to undergo some loss, for being all absorbed by too great a desire of benefitting others, for their imperfect heart is not sufficiently attentive to raise often enough its longing and love to God.

God, however, does not punish this weakness by diminishing His grace, if the laborer makes serious efforts to watch over himself and pray, and endeavors after his labor to turn his thoughts to God and seek in Him spiritual refreshment and strength. This perpetual beginning over again by intertwining the interior life with the active is very pleasing to the paternal Heart of God.

Moreover, in such an apostle, his imperfections become less deep and frequent in proportion as he learns to have recourse to Jesus without growing weary. God is ever ready to say to him, "Come back, poor weary, panting, thirsty creature, because of thy many labors; come to draw from the living waters of quiet and prayer fresh strength for other labors and sacrifices. Withdraw for a time from the crowd, for it cannot provide thee with the means thy exhausted state requires. 'Come apart from the crowd in a desert place, and rest awhile.'[78] In the calm and peace that thou shalt enjoy near me, thou shalt not only recover thy past activity, but shalt even effect more with less labor. The prophet Elijah, when wearied and discouraged, was reinvigorated by partaking of a mysterious bread. Wherefore, apostle of mine, I offer thee my grace to enable thee to turn thy thoughts to heavenly things, and renew thy intimacy with me. Come, and I will comfort thee for the sadness and disappointments thou hast experienced in thy ministry,

[78] Cf. Mark 6:31.

and in the furnace of my love, thou shalt renew thy resolutions. 'Come to me, all ye that labor and are heavily burdened, and I will refresh you.' "[79]

⁀

The interior life multiplies the apostle's energy and merits
"Thou, therefore, my son, be strong in the grace which is in Christ Jesus."[80] Grace is a participation of the life of the Man-God. A creature possesses a certain amount of power and may, in a certain sense, call itself strong. But Jesus is essential power, for in Him resides the omnipotence of the divine action. "In Thee, O Jesus," exclaims St. Gregory of Nazianzum,[81] "is all my strength." "Out of Thee, O Jesus," says St. Jerome,[82] "I am wholly powerless."

St. Bonaventure enumerates five features that the power of Jesus in us possesses: the first is to undertake difficult things and meet obstacles with courage: "Do ye manfully, and let your heart be strengthened."[83] The second is contempt of earthly things: "I have suffered the loss of all things, and count them but as dung."[84] The third is patience in tribulation: "Love is strong as death."[85] The fourth is resistance to temptation: "The Devil, as a roaring lion, goeth about . . . whom resist ye, strong in faith."[86] The fifth is

---

[79] Cf. Matt. 11:28.

[80] 2 Tim. 2:1.

[81] St. Gregory of Nazianzum (c. 329-390), Bishop of Constantinople, theologian, and Doctor.

[82] St. Jerome (c. 342-420), Doctor who translated the Bible into Latin.

[83] Ps. 30:25 (RSV = Ps. 31:24).

[84] Phil. 3:8.

[85] Cant. 8:6 (RSV = Song of Sol. 8:6).

[86] 1 Pet. 5:8-9.

the interior martyrdom — the testimony, not of blood, but of one's very life crying out to Jesus: "I wish to be all Thine." It consists in combating all concupiscence, subduing every vice, and striving energetically to acquire the virtues: "I have fought the good fight."[87]

The exterior man relies on his physical strength or natural talents; the interior man beholds in these only helps, useful indeed, but entirely insufficient. The consciousness of his own weakness, and his confidence in God's power makes known to him, as to St. Paul, the exact measure of his strength. At the sight of the obstacles in his way, he exclaims with St. Paul: "When I am weak, then am I powerful."[88]

"Without the interior life," says Pius X, "the necessary strength will be wanting for perseverance amid the annoyances and hardships of every apostolate, the coldness of men, the want of encouragement from the good, the calumnies of adversaries, and sometimes even the jealousy of friends and companions. Patience, fortitude, kindness, and considerateness are alone capable of removing or diminishing these difficulties."

Just as the sap flows from the vine into the shoots, so also, by a life of prayer, divine strength descends into the apostolic man to consolidate his understanding in the Faith. He makes progress, because this virtue casts a brighter light on his path. He advances resolutely, because he knows where he is going and how to get there.

This illumination is accompanied by so great a supernatural energy of his will that even he who has a weak and versatile character becomes capable of performing heroic actions.

[87] 2 Tim. 4:7.
[88] 2 Cor. 12:10.

Thus the "Abide in me,"[89] that is, the apostolic man's union with the Immutable, with the "Bread of the strong," explains the wonder of the invincible constancy and the perfect firmness of that admirable apostolic man St. Francis de Sales, in whom there shone an incomparable meekness united to an incomparable humility. The mind and will of the apostolic man are strengthened by his interior life, for it fortifies his charity; and Jesus gradually purifies his charity, directs and increases it, and enables it to participate in the compassion, devotedness, abnegation, and disinterestedness of His adorable Heart. We can now judge of the increased merits resulting from the ever-increasing energy of a life of prayer, for merit is proportionate to the intensity of the divine love with which actions are performed.

⁀

The interior life imparts joy and
consolation to the apostolic person

An ardent and unshaken love alone can render the apostolic life truly cheerful and pleasant, for love possesses the secret of expanding the heart, even in the midst of great sorrows and hardships. The apostolic man's life is a woof of sufferings and labors. If he does not feel sure of being loved by Jesus, how many hours of uneasiness, sadness, and gloom has he to spend, however cheerful his natural character may be! The love of Jesus Christ alone can impel the apostolic man to exclaim, like St. Paul, in his trials, "I exceedingly abound with joy in all our tribulation."[90] He can also truly say, "Amid my painful trials, the superior part of me, like that of Jesus at Gethsemani, enjoys a happiness that, although lacking

[89] John 15:4.
[90] 2 Cor. 7:4.

all sensible joy, is so great that, notwithstanding the pain and agony I feel, I would not exchange it for all human joys combined."

Come trials, contradictions, humiliations, sufferings, loss of goods, and even loss of all who are dear to him, the soul of the apostolic man now accepts these crosses far more willingly than in the beginning of his conversion. From day to day, he grows in charity. His love may not be very conspicuous; the Lord may treat him as one who is strong and lead him to a humility always deeper and deeper, or through the arduous path of expiation for his own delinquencies and those of others. It matters but little; he will gladly submit. Love favored by recollection and nourished by the Eucharist ceases not to grow, as is proved by the generosity with which the soul sacrifices and surrenders itself, without heeding the labors and hardships in seeking the souls entrusted to his apostolate, with a patience, a prudence, a tact, a compassion, and an ardor that can be explained only by the fact that he is thoroughly penetrated by the life of Christ: "But Christ liveth in me."

The sacrament of love is also that of joy. The soul cannot be interior without being devoted to the Eucharist, without intimately tasting the Gift of God and enjoying and relishing the presence and possession of its adored Beloved.

The life of the apostolic man is necessarily a life of prayer. The Curé d'Ars says, "The life of prayer is our great happiness here below. O beautiful life! Beautiful is the union of the soul with our Lord! Eternity will not suffice fully to understand this happiness. The interior life is a bath of love into which the soul plunges from Him; and he rejoices also in procuring for himself an assurance of progress in virtue and of eternal glory."

It is also a nourishment of joy for the apostolic man to labor faithfully, in order to cause his beloved Savior to be served and honored by others. Making use of his labors to increase his love for

Him, he feels his joy and consolation increasing at the same time. As "a hunter of souls," he rejoices at being able to contribute to the salvation of persons who would otherwise have been lost and, at the same time, to please God by giving Him hearts that would otherwise have been eternally separated from Him; and he rejoices also in procuring for himself an assurance of progress in virtue and of eternal glory.

The interior life refines purity of intention

The man of faith judges the works of the active life differently from him who lives only an exterior life, for he considers them in the divine plan and in their supernatural effects.

He therefore looks upon himself as a mere instrument in God's hands; he shrinks with horror from taking complacency in his own abilities, for he is persuaded of his own impotence and places all his hopes of success in God's help alone. In this manner, he remains firm in his surrender to God. Hence, in the midst of difficulties, how different is his attitude from that of the apostolic man who has not acquired intimacy with Jesus by prayer!

On the other hand, his self-surrender to God does not in the least diminish his ardor in his active labors. He acts as though success depended entirely on his efforts, but in fact, at the same time, he places his whole dependence solely on God. He finds no difficulty in subordinating all his projects and hopes to the incomprehensible designs of the Almighty, who often utilizes, for the good of souls, reverses as well as successes. He is always ready to say:

> O my God, Thy will be done concerning my labors,
> whether they prove successful or end in failure.

I limit myself to labor faithfully and generously,
without anxiety to make strenuous efforts to succeed,
but I leave to Thee alone the care of deciding whether
success or failure will procure to Thee the greater glory.
May Thy holy and adorable will be a thousand times blessed,
and may I, with the help of Thy grace, be able to
thrust back the least symptoms of complacency,
if success crowns my labors, and to humble myself
and adore Thy Providence, if Thou judgest proper
to annihilate the fruit of my labors.

In fact, the heart of the apostolic man bleeds when he beholds the tribulations of the Church. But how differently does the apostle suffer who is not animated with a supernatural spirit, for when he meets with difficulties, he becomes impatient and despondent, and even falls into despair, when his hopes are shattered. The true apostolic man makes a good use of every occurrence, success, and reverse, to increase his hopes and dilate his soul in a confiding self-surrender to Providence. Every feature of his apostolate induces him to make an act of faith; every moment of labor is for him an occasion of proving his charity, for by habitually watching over his heart, he performs every action with a purity of intention, ever more and more perfect and free from all personal views.

Wherefore each of his actions is more and more impregnated with the characteristics of holiness, and his love of souls, which in the beginning was imperfect, is daily more and more purified, until it considers in them only Jesus Christ, so that he can say with St. Paul, "My little children, of whom I am in labor again, until Christ be formed in you."[91]

[91] Gal. 4:19.

Inner Strength for Active Apostles

≈

The interior life is a protection against discouragement
"When God wills that a work should be all His," says Bossuet, "He first reduces all engaged in it to impotency and nothingness, and then He acts." This saying is incomprehensible to the apostle who does not know in what consists the soul of his apostolate. Nothing wounds God more than pride. In striving after success, he who lacks a pure intention can go so far as to make of himself a kind of deity, as the principle and end of his works. This idolatry of self is a horror to God. Wherefore, when He beholds the apostolic man neglecting to refer all his labors to the divine glory, He withdraws therefrom and allows them all to fail entirely.

The active, intelligent, and devoted apostolic workman sets himself to labor with all the ardor of his nature. Perhaps he has already had some brilliant success and even takes great complacency therein, for it was his work — yes, *his* work! And he says with Caesar, "I came, I saw, I conquered," and with him he exults!

But let us wait. Some event permitted by God, or a direct action of Satan or of the world, befalls the work or the workman himself, and the whole work is totally ruined! But there is something still more lamentable: the interior ravages consequent on the sadness and discouragement of yesterday's valiant hero! The more exuberant had his joy been, the deeper now is his despondency!

Our Lord alone could raise up these ruins. "Arise," He says to the despondent workman, "instead of attempting to do that work alone, take it up again with me, through me, and in me." But the unfortunate workman no longer heeds that voice, for he is so absorbed in the mere external part of his ministry that he scarcely ever takes into account the power and providence of God.

On the other hand, the true apostle is convinced that prayer and holiness of life are the two powerful means of successfully acting on the Heart of God and on the hearts of men. He toils gen-erously, but the mirage of success does not appear to be worthy of all his aims. Let squalls come; it matters but little to him which are their second causes. In the midst of the injury and devastation resulting therefrom, knowing that he had worked for God, he seems to hear in his heart the voice of Jesus saying the "Fear not," that, during the storm, restored peace and security to the Apos-tles; and the result of his trial is a fresh burst of confiding love for Jesus in the Eucharist and a renewal of his devotion to Our Lady of Sorrows. His spirit, far from being crushed by his want of success, comes forth reinvigorated, for "as the eagle, thy youth shall be renewed."[92] Whence has he the attitude of a successful man after the failure, the destruction of his labors? It can come alone from his union with Jesus, and his unshaken confidence in Christ's omni-potence, which inspired St. Ignatius[93] to say, "If the Society [of Jesus] were to be suppressed without any fault of mine, a quarter of an hour's communing with God would enable me to recover calm and peace." "The heart of the interior man," says the Curé d'Ars, "when in the midst of humiliations and sufferings, is like an immovable rock in mid-ocean."

Would that every apostle were animated with the sentiments that the pious General de Sonis expressed in his beautiful daily prayer:

O my God, behold in Thy presence a
poor, insignificant, helpless creature!
Plunged in my nothingness,
I prostrate myself before Thee.

[92] Cf. Ps. 102:5 (RSV = Ps. 103:5).
[93] St. Ignatius of Loyola (1491-1556), founder of the Jesuit Order.

I wish I had an offering to make Thee,
but I am naught but misery,
and Thou art my all, my riches.

My God, I thank Thee for having willed
that I should be nothing in Thy sight.
I love my humiliation, my nothingness.
I thank Thee for or having deprived me
of certain satisfactions of self-love,
of certain consolations of affection.
I thank Thee for the deceptions, ingratitude,
and humiliations that have befallen me.
They were necessary to keep me
from straying away from Thee.

O my God, be Thou blessed
when Thou sendest me trials.
I love to be consumed,
broken, destroyed by Thee.
Reduce me more and more to
nothingness. May I be in the edifice,
not the polished stone, but the grain of sand
picked up in the dust of the road.

My God, I thank Thee for having
given me a taste of Thy consolations
and for having deprived me of them.
Whatever Thou dost is just and good.
I bless Thee in my indigence; my only regret
is not to have loved Thee enough.
I desire nothing but the
accomplishment of Thy adorable will.

Thou art my Lord, and I am Thy property.
Turn me over and over again;
destroy me and mold me.
I wish to be reduced to nothingness for Thy sake.
O Jesus, how good and kind is Thy treatment of me,
even when the trial is most painful to me!
May I be crucified, but crucified by Thee. Amen.

The apostolic man has his sufferings indeed. The injury done to his work, its ruinous results in the loss of some of the souls he was striving to save. Such an occurrence, although very painful and discouraging, will not extinguish the true shepherd's ardor, but will urge him to begin again with fresh fervor. He knows that the salvation of every soul is a great work to be wrought especially by suffering. The certainty that trials generously borne will promote his progress in holiness and procure greater glory to God suffices to keep up his zeal.

Part Four

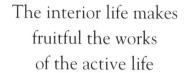

The interior life makes fruitful the works of the active life

Chapter Nine

The apostolate calls for
prayer and good example

The interior life is the condition of the fertility of the works of the active life. We do not treat here of the fecundity of the sacraments, as such, for it is derived *ex opere operato*.[94] Here we treat of the effects resulting from the labors of the apostolic man. Let us recall that if the apostolic man "abides in Christ and Christ in him," the fruitfulness willed by God is assured, for Christ says of him, "he bears much fruit."[95] It is the evident result of his interior life.

"Let those who have an intense craving for apostolic labors," says St. John of the Cross, "who imagine they can stir up the world by their preaching and other good works of zeal, reflect for a moment. They will then easily understand that they will be more useful to the Church and more pleasing to the Lord, not to mention the good example they would give to those around them, if they

---

[94] " 'By the very fact of the action's being performed,' i.e., by virtue of the saving work of Christ, accomplished once for all. It follows that the sacrament is not wrought by the righteousness of either the celebrant or the recipient, but by the power of God" (*Catechism of the Catholic Church*, par. 1128).

[95] John 15:5.

would devote more time to prayer and the exercises of the interior life. In such a condition, they would effect more good with greater ease and less labor by devoting themselves to one work, than they now do by the many they endeavor to carry on, for then mental prayer would obtain for them the graces they need to produce such fruits. Without mental prayer, all they do amounts to mere noise, resembling the striking of a hammer on an anvil and causing only an echo all around, effecting usually nothing good, or even doing harm. May God preserve us from such a laborer, if ever he happens to swell with pride! In vain are appearances in his favor; the truth is that he will effect nothing, for it is certain that no good work can be accomplished without the help of God. Oh, what sad things could be written of those who give up the interior life and aspire to perform striking things to please men and draw attention to themselves. Such laborers practically know nothing of 'the source of living water and the mysterious fountain imparting fertility.' "

We cannot accuse St. John of the Cross of exaggeration, for, as Bossuet, a competent judge, declares the saint is noted for his perfect, good, and practical common sense, for his zeal in warning his readers against using extraordinary means of sanctification, and for his remarkable precision in his writings. We will now examine some of the causes of the fecundity of the interior life.

Chapter Ten

The interior life draws God's blessing

"I will fill the soul of the priests with fatness, and thy people shall be filled with good things."[96] God does not say, "I will give my priests more zeal, more talent," but, "I will fill them with fatness" — that is, "I will fill them with my spirit and impart choice graces to them, in order that my people shall be filled with good things," that is, "with spiritual things." God can distribute His graces as He pleases, but according to the ordinary course of His Providence, He distributes them in proportion to the piety of the apostle and the dispositions of the people.

"Without me," says Christ, "you can do nothing." On Calvary He shed His redeeming Blood. But how did God assure its first fecundity? By the miracle of the diffusion of the interior life, when on Pentecost the Holy Spirit descended on the Apostles. Before that event, there was nothing narrower than the zeal and the ideal of the Apostles. But on that day, the Holy Spirit transformed them into interior men, and at once their preaching converted thousands. God does not usually renew this prodigy, but subjects the graces of sanctification to the creature's free and laborious cooperation with

96 Jer. 31:14.

actual grace. But by choosing Pentecost as the official birthday of the Church, He wishes us to understand that His priests and other apostles should prelude their apostolic works by their own personal sanctification. Wherefore every apostle should expect more fruit from his prayers and sacrifices than from his personal labor, for "it is God who giveth the increase," as St. Paul declares.[97]

Hence, Lacordaire,[98] before preaching, was wont to spend a long time in prayer and to scourge himself. Monsabre, before ascending the pulpit, would say the Rosary, kneeling. In acting as they did, these two holy and eloquent religious followed the teaching of St. Bonaventure: "The real success of an apostolate is found at the foot of the crucifix, rather than in the display of brilliant qualities."

"As to preaching, giving good example, and prayer, the greatest and most powerful of these three is prayer," says St. Bernard. This saying of St. Bernard is a commentary on the declaration of the Apostles: "As for us, we will give ourselves continually to prayer and to the ministry of the word."[99] They looked upon prayer as being of greater importance than preaching, and as being an indispensable preparation for fruitful preaching.

Our Lord Jesus Christ Himself informs us that, in importance, prayer holds the first place, for "the harvest is great, and the laborers are few." But how can this state of things be remedied? The only remedy He gives is prayer. "Pray ye, therefore, the Lord of the harvest, that He send forth laborers into the harvest."[100] If the

---

[97] Cf. 1 Cor. 3:6.

[98] Jean-Baptiste-Henri Dominique Lacordaire (1802-1861), French Dominican noted for his great preaching.

[99] Acts 6:4.

[100] Matt. 9:37-38.

mere supplication of a holy soul is a more powerful means of remedying the want of laborers than any other, it follows that the fruitfulness of the zealous apostle depends principally on his being a man of prayer.

The first requisite in an apostle is prayer. The next is "to preach, to labor." Pope Pius X in his encyclical of June 11, 1905, to the bishops of Italy, says, "To restore all things in Christ by the apostolate, divine grace is indispensable, and the apostle receives it only under the condition of being united to Christ. It is only after forming Jesus Christ in ourselves that we shall be easily able to restore Him to the family and to society. All those who participate in the apostolate must therefore possess genuine piety."[101]

What we assert of prayer is to be applied to all the other elements of the interior life, such as sufferings — that is, all that is interiorly or exteriorly painful to nature. Some men suffer as pagans, others as reprobates, and others again as saints. To suffer truly with Christ, we must suffer as saints, and then our suffering will profit us personally and will be capable of applying to men's souls the mystery of the Passion; and we may then truly say with St. Paul, "I fill up those things that are wanting of the sufferings of Christ, in my flesh, for His body, which is the Church."[102] These words of St. Paul are explained by St. Augustine as follows: "The sufferings of Christ were complete, but in our [divine] Head only; but in His mystical members they are still incomplete." Christ suffered, first, as our Head; and now it is the turn of His Mystical Body to suffer. Every priest, every apostle can say, "I am a member of Christ, and that which is wanting to the sufferings of Christ I must endeavor to complete by my sufferings for the Church, His Mystical Body."

---

[101] *Fermo Proposito* (On Catholic Action in Italy), no. 11.
[102] Col. 1:24.

Inner Strength for Active Apostles

According to Father Faber, the fecundity of the apostolic works may be ascribed to the union of the sacrifices of the apostles to the Sacrifice of the Cross, and thereby to their participation in the efficacy of the Blood of Christ shed on Calvary.

Chapter Eleven

The apostle sanctifies
others through his interior life

In the Sermon on the Mount, our divine Savior says to His Apostles, "You are the salt of the earth; you are the light of the world."[103] We are the salt of the earth in proportion to our holiness; but "if the salt lose its savor," of what use is it? It is only fit to be cast out into the way and trampled upon.

But the pious apostle is truly the salt of the earth, a real agent of preservation from the corruption of human society. He is a shining light in the night of error, for the brightness of his example, more than his preaching, will dispel the darkness accumulated by the spirit of the world, and cause the ideal of true happiness, which Jesus Christ traced in the Eight Beatitudes, to reign in the hearts of the objects of his labor. That which is most capable of inducing the faithful to lead a truly Christian life is precisely the virtue of him who has to teach it. On the other hand, his weaknesses turn men away from God. "Through you the name of God is blasphemed among the Gentiles."[104] Wherefore, the apostle should on

---

[103] Matt. 5:13, 14.
[104] Cf. Rom. 2:24.

every occasion show the lighted torch of his good example rather than regale men with fine speeches; that is, he should take great care to practice what he preaches.

It has been aptly remarked that a physician can take proper care of the health of his patients, and cure them, even if he is ill himself; but to succeed in curing souls, we should have a healthy soul, for in this matter, the spiritual physician must impart something of himself, at least by his example. Men have the right to be exacting from him who pretends to reform them, and they soon discern whether the reformer's actions agree with his teaching, or if his preaching is only deceptive speech.

How powerful, for instance, is the priest's preaching on prayer if the people often witness him communing with our divine Savior in the tabernacle! How persuasive he will be when preaching on avoiding idleness, on doing penance, if he is always usefully employed and mortified! And if he is ever kind, charitable to all, even to the poor and to children, as a true imitator of Jesus Christ, how deeply will his exhortations sink into the hearts of his hearers, "whose pattern he is"![105]

The teacher who is not an interior man considers that he has done his duty if he merely hears and explains the lessons of his pupils. If he were an interior man, a saying escaping from his heart, an expressive gesture or look, his very demeanor, his very manner of making the Sign of the Cross, of reciting the prayers before and at the end of class or school, might produce as good an impression as a good sermon!

A Sister in a hospital or in another institution possesses a power and an efficacious means of doing much good without transgressing the limits of duty, for she can inspire in the hearts

[105] Cf. 1 Pet. 5:3.

of those entrusted to her care the love of Jesus Christ and His Church.

The Christian religion has been propagated, not so much by long and frequent discussions and learned explanations, as by the works of a truly Christian life of the apostolic men and of the faithful, a life so contrary to the worldly spirit of selfishness and sensuality. If now the Catholics, or at least all the apostles, were as holy as the early Christians, how irresistible would their apostolate be among our modern pagans and the sects that are so prejudiced against our holy Church and her doctrine!

O external radiation of an interior soul united to God, how powerful art thou! It was the sight of the Venerable Father Passerat,[106] saying Mass so devoutly that drew Father Desurmont to the Congregation of the Most Holy Redeemer, which he was destined to illustrate and benefit so greatly. The faithful possess an intuition of holiness that nothing can deceive, for they flock from all sides to obscure men of God, as we see in the case of St. Clement Hofbauer,[107] the Curé d'Ars, and many others.

It is to the apostles especially that Jesus Christ says, "So let your light shine before men, that they may see your good works and glorify your Father who is in Heaven,"[108] by imitating them. St. Paul addresses this admonition to them also: "In all things, show thyself an example of good works."[109] "Be thou an example of the faithful in word, in conversation, in charity, in faith, in chastity."[110] "The

---

[106] Venerable Joseph Passerat (1772-1858), French Redemptorist priest who founded Redemptorist houses in many countries.

[107] St. Clement Hofbauer (1751-1820), Austrian Redemptorist priest named Apostle and Patron to Vienna.

[108] Matt. 5:16.

[109] Titus 2:7.

[110] 1 Tim. 4:12.

things which you have . . . seen in me, these do ye."[111] "Be followers of me, as I also am of Christ."[112] We should be able to challenge our adversaries as Christ did the Pharisees: "Which of you shall convince me of sin?"[113] for we are called to imitate Him: "Jesus began to do and to teach."[114] Therefore it behooves the apostle to follow St. Paul's admonition: "Carefully study to present thyself approved unto God, a workman that need not be ashamed."[115]

Pope Leo XIII says, "Above all, very dear sons, bear in mind that the indispensable condition of true zeal and the best pledge of success is purity and holiness of life."[116] And Pope Pius X says likewise, "All who are devoted to Catholic works should be men of such a spotless life, as to be fit to serve as an efficacious example to all men."

---

[111] Phil. 4:9.

[112] 1 Cor. 11:1.

[113] John 8:46.

[114] Acts 1:1.

[115] Cf. 2 Tim. 2:15.

[116] *Depuis le jour* (On the education of the clergy), September 8, 1899.

Chapter Twelve

The apostle radiates holiness

One of the most serious obstacles to the conversion of men is that God is "a hidden God."[117] Nevertheless, God, by an effect of His goodness, discloses Himself to men through His saints and through saintly souls. Through such persons the supernatural pierces and enables the faithful to perceive "something of the mystery of God." May it not be the brightness of sanctity, the splendor of the divine influx, what the theologians call sanctifying grace, or better still, the result of the ineffable presence of the Holy Spirit dwelling in holy souls? In fact, this divine presence spiritualizes such souls still more. Just as the sun's rays passing through a crystal vase render it still more sparkling, so also the indwelling of the Holy Spirit in very holy souls renders them more luminous and enables them to spread grace and charity around them.

The manifestation of the divine, which was perceivable in all the actions and motions and even in the sleep of the Man-God, is, in some degree, to be perceivable also in persons leading a very intense interior life. The wonderful conversions wrought by certain saints through the renown of their virtue, the numerous aspirants

[117] Isa. 45:15.

to perfect life who flocked from diverse places seeking admission into their communities, proclaimed in an evident manner the secret power of the silent apostolate. The sanctity of the abbot St. Anthony[118] attracted the numerous monks that peopled the Egyptian deserts. The sanctity of St. Benedict drew together the vast army of Benedictines, who civilized Europe; that of St. Bernard exercised an unparalleled influence over monarchs and peoples. St. Vincent Ferrer's[119] holiness aroused an indescribable enthusiasm wherever he went and the conversion of immense multitudes. And the holiness of St. Ignatius enlists in the service of the Church an army of defenders and apostles, such as St. Francis Xavier, who, by his labors and virtues, conquered to Christ and His Church more than a million pagans. These and other prodigies can be explained only by the power of God shining through the holy life of His apostolic men.

It is a misfortune for important apostolic works when there is a lack of men of interior life engaged therein, for then the supernatural agency is as if enchained and powerless, and gradually the religious spirit will decline in that region, and the wicked will possess more power to do harm.

Although St. John Baptist performed no miracle, multitudes were attracted to him. The voice of the Curé d'Ars was too weak to be heard by the crowds around him. Although they were unable to understand what he said, they could see him, and the very sight of him subdued them and converted them. A lawyer returning from Ars, being asked what had struck him the most, replied, "I have seen God in a man."

---

[118] St. Anthony (251-356), desert monk and father of Western monasticism.

[119] St. Vincent Ferrer (1350-1419), Dominican mission preacher who helped mend the Great Schism of the West.

This reminds us of an apt comparison. A person standing on an insulated stool and holding a wire connected with an electric machine, becomes charged with electricity if he is touched by a person standing by; there is an electric spark emitted from him that produces a shock in the one who touches him. In like manner, the interior man is united to or connected with God and so filled with His Spirit that all who come in contact with him are touched, as it were, by the Spirit of God dwelling in him, so that we may say of the interior man what the Evangelist says of our divine Savior: "All the multitude sought to touch Him, for virtue went out from Him."[120] The words and acts of the interior life are as the outflow of that latent and supreme power for removing and overthrowing obstacles and effecting conversions, or increasing fervor. The more deeply rooted the theological virtues are in a heart, the more their outflow promotes their birth in the souls of others.

By his interior life, the apostle radiates Faith. The presence of God in him is manifest to those who hear him. Like St. Bernard, he isolates himself and constructs for himself an interior solitude, in which he enjoys the company of a mysterious and loved Guest, with whom he communes at every moment, who inspires his words, counsels, and directions. Men feel convinced that he is supported and guided by Him, and that his words are but the faithful echo of those of his interior Guest, and that he, therefore, speaks "as the words of God."[121] It is the Divine Word teaching, speaking by His creature, so that he may, like Jesus Christ, say, "The words that I speak to you, I speak not of myself."[122] The influence of the words of an interior man, of a man of God, is far more potent than that

[120] Luke 6:19.
[121] 1 Pet. 4:11.
[122] John 14:10.

of one who lacks the interior spirit. The latter may interest and charm, but is unable of itself to lead to a supernatural faith or cause men "to live by faith."[123]

Never before has there been so much aching, so many arguments and explanations, so many fine treatises on faith, and, we regret to say it, never before has there been less "living by faith." Many catechists seem to consider the act of faith only as an act of the intellect, although it pertains also to the will. They forget that to have faith is a supernatural gift, and that between perceiving the motives of credibility and the act of faith itself, there is an immense distance, which can be filled only by God together with the goodwill of the person taught. To fill up this void, the holiness of the teacher reflecting the divine light contributes not a little influence in moving the will of the person taught.

The interior life of the apostle radiates hope

Being firmly convinced, by faith, that true happiness can be found only in God alone, he is able to speak so sweetly and consolingly of Heaven and its joys and rewards, and thereby induce those afflicted with trials and sufferings to bear them cheerfully, especially after they have received Jesus in the Holy Eucharist. How lively and penetrating are the words of consolation from one who can truly apply to himself these words of St. Paul: "Our conversation is in Heaven."[124] Others may make fine literary and poetic descriptions of heavenly rewards, but their words will produce no practical results similar to those of the words of an interior man, for the latter will encourage the sorely tried and the despondent to

[123] Rom. 1:17.
[124] Phil. 3:20.

bear their heavy crosses for God's sake, with resignation and even cheerfully!

⬲

The interior apostle radiates charity

All who really wish to sanctify themselves desire above all to possess charity, for "the abiding in Jesus and of Jesus in oneself" is the object of every interior man. If preaching in missions and retreats on the eternal truths is indispensable and salutary, the preaching on the love of Jesus for us produces generally in us a more salutary and lasting impression. If the preacher is himself an interior man and truly loves God, his words will convert his hearers. When there is question of withdrawing a soul from sin or raising it from fervor to perfection, the love of Jesus is the incomparable lever. The Christian wallowing in the mire of evil habits, but still capable of recognizing in others their ardent love of God and the void and deception of earthly loves, commences to experience disgust for the latter. He already appreciates to some extent the immense love of Jesus for men and the possibility of loving Him in return with a love above all love for creatures. Through the exhortations of an interior apostle, such a sinner will be induced to make all the sacrifices necessary to cause the love of Jesus to reign in his heart.

⬲

The interior apostle radiates kindness

"A zeal that is not kind," says St. Francis de Sales, "proceeds from a false charity." By making mental prayer on Him whom the Church invokes as the "Ocean of Goodness," we can succeed in reforming and transforming ourselves, however selfish and harsh we may naturally be, for our defects would gradually be corrected with the divine assistance. By nourishing ourselves frequently with the sacred flesh of Him in whom "appeared the goodness and kindness of God,"[125] and who is the image of the Father's goodness,[126] we participate in the divine goodness and kindness and experience the need of being, like Him, "diffusive." The more often our heart is united to Jesus Christ, the more it participates in His goodness, the principal quality of His divine-human Heart. The apostolic man, being transfigured, as it were, by divine love, his words and actions will bear the seal of compassionate benevolence and loving kindness toward the sinful and the lowly, and with an ever-increasing generosity and devotedness, he will joyfully and magnanimously, sacrifice himself for the welfare of his fellowmen, without desire of popularity, without subtle selfishness.

"God has willed," says Lacordaire, "that we can do good to men only through love, and that without love, we cannot enlighten them or inspire them with the love of virtue." In fact, man glories in resisting compulsion and in making objections to those who always pretend to convince him. But since it is not humiliating to yield to kindness, man easily yields to kind ways.

How many conversions from error, from a sinful life, are brought about by the Sisters without discussions, and only through their indefatigable devotedness and even heroic kindness! Witnessing such great charity and devotedness, the infidel, the non-Catholic, and the hardened sinner cannot forbear exclaiming in his heart, "God is there, for I see Him such as He is called — the Good God!" God must be good indeed, since communing with Him enables interior persons to suppress all self-love and natural repugnances.

---

[125] Titus 3:4.
[126] Cf. Wisd. 7:26.

"Kindness," says Father Faber, "is the overflowing of self upon others. We put others in the place of self. We treat them as we would wish to be treated ourselves. Kindness adds sweetness to everything. It is a divine, rather than a human thing, and it is human because it springs from the soul of man just at the point where the divine image was graven deepest." Elsewhere Father Faber remarks that "it is always the contemplative saints, who have loved sinners even more than the active saints, who devoted their whole life in laboring for their conversion." And this explains why an apostle should be an interior man.

"Whether you encourage or strive to deter," says St. Vincent Ferrer, "have a mother's heart; show to all . . . a tender charity, and let the sinner perceive that charity inspires your every word. If you wish to benefit souls, first have recourse to God, that He may pour into your heart charity, the abridgment of all virtues, so that it may enable you to obtain your object." There is an infinite distance between natural kindness, which is only a fruit of one's temperament, and the supernatural kindness of the soul of the apostolic man. The former may inspire respect, and even sometimes direct to him the love due to God, but it cannot induce a man, for God's sake, to make the sacrifices necessary to return to God. Such an effect can be the outcome only of a kindness flowing from intimacy with Jesus Christ, that is, from the interior life. Hence, the interior apostolic man may sometimes do things of which even very good persons would disapprove.

A certain layman, conversing one day with Pope Pius X, applied some very bitter epithets to an enemy of the Church. "My son," said the Pope, "I do not approve of your language. As a penance, listen to this anecdote. A priest I know well, when he first came to his parish, thought it his duty to visit every family in the place, not only Catholics, but also Jews, Protestants, and freemasons, and he announced from the pulpit that he would do the same every year. This caused a great agitation among the neighboring priests, and they complained of it to the bishop. The priest was summoned by the bishop and was severely reprimanded. The priest modestly replied, 'Monsignor, in the Gospel, Jesus Christ commands the shepherd to bring *all* the sheep to the fold.[127] How can I do this if I do not go to seek them? Moreover, in doing so, I do not yield any principle, for I merely show my interest and charity to every soul, even the stray ones, whom God has entrusted to me. I have announced these visits from the pulpit; if you insist on my giving them up, please give me the order in writing, so that I may know that I am guided by your orders in giving up my intended visits!'

"Moved by the correctness of the priest's views, the bishop did not insist. The sequel showed that the priest was right, for some of the stray sheep were converted, and all the others ever after showed great respect for our holy religion. We must be firm and unwavering with regard to principles, but we should extend our charity to all men, even to the worst enemies of the Church."

The interior apostle radiates humility

The humility of Jesus Christ, as well as His meekness and kindness, attracted multitudes to Him. "Without me," He says to us, "you can do nothing." Having been raised to the dignity of cooperator with Christ, the apostolic man will become the agent of supernatural operations, but under the condition that Jesus shall always be apparent therein. The more the apostle effaces himself, the more will Jesus manifest Himself. Without this self-effacement,

---

[127] John 10:16.

the apostolic man will "plant and water" in vain, and there will be no growth. Genuine humility derives its special charms from Jesus Christ, for it breathes the divine. The zealous laborer who effaces himself, in order that Jesus may appear to act, may say with St. John the Baptist, "It behooveth that He should increase, and that I should decrease."[128] Such a one will receive from Jesus the gift of winning always more and more hearts.

Humility is one of the most powerful agents in saving souls. "Believe me," avers St. Vincent de Paul to his priests, "we shall never be fit to do the work of God if we are not persuaded that, of ourselves, we are more apt to spoil than to succeed." Arrogant ways, airs of self-sufficiency are often the causes of failures in the works of the apostolate. The up-to-date Christian means to preserve his independence. He will obey no one but God; before obeying God's minister, he must first be so convinced of his duty to do so, as if he beheld God's signature to His minister's words. Hence, in his ministry, the apostolic man must efface himself by his humility, so that God alone may appear therein and cause his labors to succeed. Hence, a certain writer calls the truly humble apostle "a transparency of God," for God can be seen, as it were, through the labors of his ministry.

Humility, according to all the masters of the spiritual life, is the foundation of all the moral virtues, and is therefore absolutely necessary to the apostolic man, both for his sanctification and for the success of his labors. God hates the proud and gives His grace only to the humble. Jesus requires all men, but especially His apostolic men, to learn from Him humility: "Learn of me, because I am meek and humble of heart."[129] The apostolic man who is deficient

[128] Cf. John 3:30.
[129] Matt. 11:29.

in humility is deficient in the interior life and will effect but little for his own sanctification and for that of his neighbor.

The apostle radiates firmness and meekness
The saints have often been vehement, especially against error, the contagion of sin, and hypocrisy. St. Bernard's zeal was remarkable for its firmness. But prompted by his interior spirit, he had recourse to firmness only when it was evident that all other means would fail; and after showing a holy indignation and prescribing remedies and reparation, and requiring pledges and promises, he would, with a maternal kindness, as it were, endeavor to convert those whom his conscience urged him to combat. Although he condemned without pity the errors of Abelard, after refuting him and reducing him to silence, he treated him so kindly as to make him his friend. When principles were not at stake, Bernard did all in his power to prevent harsh measures. When he heard of the persecution of the Jews in Germany, he at once left his convent to preach a crusade of peace and showed that the only weapons to be used against the Jews are moral persuasion, good example, and devotedness.

In the Chablais, where Protestantism had first been introduced by force of arms and had, in the course of time, become deeply rooted, and all efforts to convert the inhabitants had failed, St. Francis de Sales undertook the difficult task. Their ministers, hearing of this, planned to kill him. But Francis, refusing the protection of the secular arm, went there, meek, humble, and self-sacrificing. The Calvinists beholding in him a man wholly unselfish and resplendent, as it were, with charity toward God and men, were full of admiration, flocked to hear him, and the result was that, in a few years, Francis had brought back into the Church the great majority of the people. But the meek Francis, when finding it necessary, did not hesitate to invoke the power of the secular arm to confirm the fruits of his words of meekness and of his heroic devotedness. In this he, like other saints, imitated the example of Jesus Christ.

In the Gospel, we perceive our divine Savior forgiving with the greatest kindness the penitent Magdalen, the woman taken in adultery, and the good thief. He was a friend to Zacheus. The publicans gathered around Him, and He received them and ate with them. He was gentle and kind to the sick, the afflicted, the poor, and little children. And yet the Incarnate Meekness and Kindness uses a whip to drive the venders out of the temple. And how strong and severe are his expressions when alluding to Herod and denouncing the vices and hypocrisy of the scribes and Pharisees!

Whenever principles are not at stake, it is meekness that should predominate in the evangelical laborer. "We can catch more flies with a little honey," remarks St. Francis de Sales, "than with a barrel of vinegar." When the disciples, angered at being refused hospitality, wished to call down fire from Heaven to destroy the town, our Lord rebuked them, saying, "Ye know not of what spirit you are."[130] A certain French bishop, well known for his strict adherence to principles, not long ago went to console the families in his episcopal city who were mourning over their sons who had been killed in battle. One of these families was that of a strict Calvinist, known for his great aversion to Catholics, and the bishop's kind, sympathetic words so deeply moved him that he exclaimed, "Is it possible that a bishop, so noble by birth and so distinguished for his learning, should come, notwithstanding the difference of our religions, to my poor dwelling to sympathize with me and console

[130] Luke 9:55.

me?" This fact caused him to entertain a kinder disposition toward the Catholic Church and Catholics.

The interior man radiates mortification

The spirit of mortification is necessary to fecundate the labors of the apostolic man. All is resumed in the Cross; and so long as we have not caused the mystery of the Cross to penetrate souls, we have only grazed them. But who can prevail upon weak men to accept a mystery so repugnant to man's natural horror of suffering? Only he who can say with St. Paul, "With Christ I am nailed to the Cross."[131] They can, "who always bear about in their bodies the mortification of Jesus Christ, so that the life also of Jesus may be made manifest in their bodies."[132] To mortify oneself is to reproduce what St. Paul says of Jesus: "Christ did not please Himself,"[133] and to renounce oneself, to love what does not please us, to aspire to be, without ceasing, an immolated victim. But this cannot be attained except by leading an interior life.

St. Francis of Assisi, walking in silence with eyes cast down, preached with fruit, by his very appearance, the mystery of the Cross. An unmortified man, were he as eloquent as St. John Chrysostom or Bossuet, would make no impression on men, were he to act in like manner. The world is so thoroughly impregnated with the love of pleasure and enjoyment, that no merely natural ability or eloquence can conquer it. Only the apostolic man can, by his spirit of mortification and detachment, bring the Passion home to men. St. Paul would apply the epithet "enemies of the

---

[131] Gal. 2:19.
[132] Cf. 2 Cor. 4:10.
[133] Rom. 15:3.

Cross of Christ"[134] to many Christians who behold in the Christian religion only exterior practices handed down by tradition and periodically performed with respect, but without reference to the amendment of life, to combating the passions, or to leading a life conformable to the spirit of the Gospel. Of these Jesus can say, "This people honoreth me with their lips, but their heart is far from me."[135]

"Enemies of the Cross of Christ" are the effeminate Christians who regard all the comforts of life as indispensable, who follow all the fashions of the world, enjoy inordinate pleasures, and are shocked by this saying of Jesus Christ: "Unless you do penance, you shall all likewise perish."[136] To them the Cross is a scandal.[137] And this is the kind of Christian an apostle devoid of interior life is apt to produce!

Our divine Savior desires only our heart. It was to win it, to possess our will, and to encourage us to follow Him on the way of self-denial that He came on earth to be our model and to die for us. The apostolic man, whose life is based on this teaching of Jesus, "Let him deny himself,"[138] will alone be able to inspire in men the self-denial necessary for every true Christian. But the apostolic man who follows Jesus Christ only from afar will fail in attempting to inspire self-denial in others, for "no one can give what he has not," as the saying is. Only he who possesses the practical science of Jesus crucified can oppose a strong dike against the world's constant seeking after wealth, ease, comfort, pleasure, enjoyment, and

[134] Phil. 3:18.
[135] Matt. 15:8.
[136] Luke 13:3.
[137] 1 Cor. 1:23.
[138] Matt. 16:24.

the gratification of the passions, which threaten to submerge all things and ruin families and nations.

To preach Jesus Christ crucified was the summary of St. Paul's apostolate, and because he lived according to his preaching, he was able to cause men to relish "the mystery of the Cross" and to live in accordance with it. Every apostle should, by his interior life, be able to fathom this mystery and induce men to live by its teachings. Pope Benedict XV, in his encyclical of November 1, 1914, *Ad Beatissimi Apostolorum,* exhorts apostles to plough more deeply (in cultivating the Lord's vineyard), in order to cut away from men's souls the love of ease, comfort, and pleasure, and all selfishness and frivolity, and prevent them from forgetting the goods of eternity. This is an appeal to the interior life of the ministers of the "Crucified."

Chapter Thirteen

The apostle is endowed with true eloquence

True eloquence is capable of converting souls and leading them to virtue. In the Office of St. John the Evangelist we read these words: "Leaning on the Lord's breast, he drank from the fountain flowing from the sacred breast of the Lord, and he spread the grace of the Divine Word over the whole earth." What a deep lesson in these words for those who preach, teach catechism, or have to perform some apostolic work! By these words, the Church indicates to them the source of true eloquence. The interior apostolic men who "draw the waters [of grace] from the Savior's fountains [His Sacred Heart]"[139] possess true eloquence, for they speak heavenly to earth, and enlighten, move, console, and strengthen their hearers. The apostolic man who relies on his mental prayer, his Mass, his holy Communion, and his visit to the Blessed Sacrament and the Blessed Virgin for the success of his apostolate will possess an eloquence that will bear fruit, and he who does not so rely will be but "sounding brass and a tinkling cymbal,"[140] for he is not a fit

[139] Isa. 12:3.
[140] 1 Cor. 13:1.

115

channel of that love which renders the eloquence of the friends of God irresistible. "As to those who are not wont to commune with God," said Pope Pius X in his exhortation of August 4, 1908, to the Catholic clergy, "when they speak of Him to men or impart directions for a Christian life, they lack entirely the divine inspiration, so that the word of God seems to be almost dead in them. Their speech, however brilliant for its prudence and [natural] eloquence, does not at all represent the language of the Good Shepherd, which the sheep willingly listen to; it makes only a noise and melts away into nothingness."[141]

Let us again bear in mind that only the Holy Spirit, the Principle of all spiritual fecundity, effects conversions and imparts the graces that enable men to flee sin and practice virtue. The word of the evangelical laborer, when penetrated by the unction of the Holy Spirit, becomes a living channel of fecundation for souls. Before Pentecost, the preaching of the Apostles had but little result. After their retreat of ten days wholly spent in the exercises of the interior life, the Holy Spirit came down and, as it were, took possession of them and transformed them. Their first essays in preaching were truly miraculous draughts. The same is the case with evangelical sowers; they plant and water with great efficacy, and the Holy Spirit always gives the increase. Their preaching is both the sowing of the seed and the rain fecundating it; and the sun, which giveth the increase, is never wanting.

The apostolic man derives his eloquence from his life of union with Christ through prayer and the custody of his heart, and also from Holy Scripture, which he studies diligently and of which he is very fond. Every word of God to man, every word from the lips of Jesus is as a diamond to him. He never opens Scripture until he has

---

[141] *Haerent Animo* (On priestly sanctity).

prayed for the Holy Spirit to enlighten him. Watch with how great an unction he quotes the word of God when preaching, and what a difference between the light he draws from it and the learned or ingenuous applications made therefrom by the mere light of human reason! The former exhibits the living truth capable of enlightening and imparting life to the hearers, and leading them to virtue. But the latter may please and cause admiration without, however, leading to salvation.

The interior life, to be complete, requires a tender devotion to Mary Immaculate, for she is the channel of grace, and especially of all choice graces. The apostolic man, who is accustomed to have constant recourse to the Mother of the Author of grace, exerts a powerful influence in his labors, not only when he speaks of her grandeur, privileges and unlimited power with God, and of her love for men, especially for poor sinners, but also when he seeks to inspire his hearers with a tender devotion to her and great confidence in her perpetual help in all wants, especially in temptation and at the hour of death.

Chapter Fourteen

⁀

The interior apostolic
man produces lasting results

As we have seen, only an interior laborer can produce interior men. Hence, to produce permanent or lasting effects, we must seek to make interior men of those for whom we labor. Fervor may, at first, be very great in a sodality, in a religious community, or in a religious order, but if the members are not interior men, that fervor will not last, but will soon begin to diminish, until it becomes extinct. On the other hand, associations whose members are interior men will live for centuries in their first fervor and always prove exemplary and useful. We will not allude here to pious associations, very numerous and fervent at first, that in a few years gradually dwindle down to a few members. But there are still in existence in France prosperous works, or associations, founded before the old French Revolution by priests who lacked all the natural qualities calculated to ensure success, and had only their genuine piety and ardent zeal for the glory of God to recommend them.

One of these works, or associations, at Marseilles, cared for students and workmen. Its founder, the Abbe Allemand, required of all the young members as holy a life as was led by the early

Christians; and ever since, the youthful apostles, for so we may call them, have continued and are still doing their grand work and have given to the Church numerous bishops, priests, religious, and missionaries, and to society thousands of exemplary and useful fathers of families, who are the support of the Church and ornaments in every walk of life.

An example, among many, will show the difference between the result of the work of an interior apostle and that of the work of one apparently more popular who was not an interior man, or who was far less so than the first. A certain holy religious, deceased not many years ago, but whose life has been published, was director of a congregation of very capable Catechist Sisters. This interior man said one day to the superior of one of the convents: "Methinks it would be well for Sister X. to cease teaching catechism for a whole year at least."

"But, Reverend Father," replied Mother Superior, "you seem not to know that she is our best teacher and directress. The children come in crowds from all parts of the city, being attracted to the catechism classes by her wonderful ability in teaching and managing them. If we should remove her, most of the little boys would cease attending the catechism lessons."

"I have assisted at some of her lessons," replied the priest. "She indeed dazzles and entertains the children, but in too human a manner. She will, after spending another year in the novitiate, be better grounded in the interior life and will be also better able to sanctify her soul and the souls of the children by her zeal and talents. But she is at present actually an obstacle to the direct action of our Lord on the souls of the children preparing for their First Holy Communion. But as I see my proposition does not please you, I will agree on a compromise. I know Sister N. as a very interior soul, although not very talented. Ask your superior general to send her to you for a time; and at first let Sister X. start the cate-chism class for a quarter of an hour, just to calm your fears con-cerning the desertion of the children; and later on there will be no need of her making her appearance at all. You shall then see that the children will pray better and sing more devoutly, for their rec-ollection and docility will be far more satisfactory."

Sister N. came, and two weeks later, Sister N. alone taught the children catechism, and the number of children attending the class continued to increase. It was evident that it was Jesus who was teaching them through her, for by her looks, her modesty, her meekness, and her kindness, and by the way she pronounced the Savior's name and made the Sign of the Cross, she made a deep and reverential impression on the children. Sister X. had shown great talent in explaining and making interesting subjects that are usually dry to children.

But Sister N. did more than prepare well her explanations and adapt them to the capacity of the children; for what predominated in her teaching was the unction that accompanied all she said and did. And it is by the unction that souls come into real contact with Jesus Christ. In Sister N.'s classes, there was far less noisy demon-stration and none of that fascination that the lecture of some great explorer or weird storyteller would provoke. On the other hand, there was an atmosphere of recollection, for the boys behaved in the classroom as well as if they were in church during divine ser-vice, and no human means were used to prevent dissipation of mind or signs of weariness.

The influence hovering over the class was that of Jesus, for an interior person explaining the catechism is like the heavenly tones of a musical instrument played by Jesus Himself, and no hu-man art, however marvelous, is comparable to the action of Jesus on souls.

⌒

Through the Holy Eucharist, the interior life
resumes all the fecundity of the apostolate

"The end of the Incarnation and of every apostolate," says St. Augustine, "is to render human nature divine." "The only-begotten Son of God," says St. Thomas, "wishing to make us partakers of His divine nature, assumed our human nature, in order that, having become man, He might make men gods."

It is in the eucharistic life, that is, in the solid interior life nourished in the Divine Banquet, that the apostolic man assimilates the divine life, so to speak, for our divine Savior declares, "Except you eat the flesh of the Son of man and drink His Blood, you cannot have life in you."[142] The eucharistic life is the life of Jesus in us, not only by the indispensable state of grace, but by the superabundance of its action in us, for Jesus says, "I am come that they may have life, and may have it more abundantly."[143]

If the apostolic man should overabound in divine life, that he may impart it to the faithful, and if he finds it so abundantly only in the blessed Eucharist, how can he expect fruits from his labor, unless through the Eucharist? We cannot meditate on the consequences of the dogma of the Real Presence, of the Holy Sacrifice of the Mass and Holy Communion, without being led to the conclusion that our divine Savior instituted this sacrament, as the focus of all the activity and devotedness of every apostolate truly useful to the Church. If the whole Redemption gravitates around Calvary, all the graces of this mystery flow from the altar. And the apostle who does not live thereby, possesses only a lifeless speech incapable of imparting salvation, since it does not emanate from a

[142] John 6:54.
[143] John 10:10.

heart sufficiently impregnated with the redeeming Blood of the Savior.

Jesus Christ had a special end in view when, after the Last Supper, He so emphatically and so precisely declared, by the parable of the vine and its branches, the inefficacy of an action that is not animated by the interior spirit. "As the branch cannot of itself bear fruit, so also neither can you, unless you abide in me." Then, to show the power of an apostolic man united to Him by his interior life, He adds, "He that abideth in me and I in him, he bringeth forth much fruit."[144] The interior man, and he only, bears much fruit, for it is only through such a one that God acts powerfully. Hence, St. Athanasius[145] exclaims, "Through the Flesh of Jesus Christ we have become [as] gods." When the preacher or catechist preserves in himself the warmth of the divine Blood, when his heart is enkindled with the fire that consumes the eucharistic Heart of Jesus, how living, ardent, and inflamed are his words and capable of communicating his ardor to his hearers, for through Holy Communion his words become as "Christbearers" to others! When Satan retains souls in ignorance, when that proud and unclean spirit strives to fill souls with pride, in order to drown them in the mire of vice, the blessed Eucharist, the life of the interior man, enables the apostolic man to triumph in himself and others over the enemy of salvation.

Love is perfected by the Eucharist. This loving "Memorial of the Passion" re-enkindles in the soul of the apostolic man the fire of divine love when it is in danger of going out and enables him, by the consideration of Gethsemani, the Praetorium, and Calvary, to speak to the suffering and the afflicted in words that will enable

[144] Cf. John 15:4, 5.
[145] St. Athanasius (c. 297-373), Bishop of Alexandria and Doctor.

them to participate in the consolations derived from the thought of Jesus crucified. Like the saints, the apostolic man should frequently visit Jesus in the Blessed Sacrament to seek light and strength, to recommend to Him his labors for souls. He will make progress in the interior life only in proportion to his love of the Eucharist and his zeal in inspiring it in those entrusted to his charge. Pope Pius X, the pope of frequent and even daily Communion, chose as his motto "to reestablish all things in Christ"[146] and judged that the chief means of ensuring its success is the grafting of the eucharistic life in both the clergy and the faithful. The ravages in the past of unbelief, indifference, and crime, in spite of so many able and zealous apostles, can be attributed in great part to the insufficiency of their eucharistic life.

Let us, therefore, we apostles, show our ardent love for Jesus in the Eucharist, often visit Him, and do all in our power to promote among the faithful daily attendance at holy Mass, and frequent and even daily Communion. Let us take to heart these words of St. Francis of Assisi: "Mental prayer is the source of grace. Preaching is the channel for distributing the grace we have received from Heaven. The ministers of the Word of God have been chosen by Him to carry to all nations what they themselves have learned and gathered from the Lord, especially when *before the tabernacle*." Let us follow the saint's directions, and we shall be able to contribute our share toward "reestablishing all things in Christ."

---

[146] Eph. 1:10.

Part Five

Living the interior life

Chapter Fifteen

Daily mental prayer

Our zeal, to be efficacious, stands in need of the assistance of Jesus Christ in such a manner that, in all we do, Jesus is the chief agent, and we are only instruments in His hands. Jesus will not bless our labors if we put our trust in ourselves or in mere natural means. "We should labor so earnestly, as if success depended entirely on our efforts," says St. Alphonsus, "and at the same time, we must put our whole trust in God, who alone can give us success in our apostolate." But we cannot expect God's assistance or blessing in our labors if self-love is our object, instead of the love of God.

It is our sacred duty to engage in the works to which God calls us. We should not seek to have our own way and work independently of God or of our lawful superiors who hold His place in our regard. We should so perform the duties of our apostolate that, far from injuring our interior life, they may always promote it. We should never so overburden ourselves with work as to be unable to perform our spiritual exercises, for they are the food of our soul, necessary to maintain its strength and spiritual life. The more we have to do, the more also will be our need of the strength imparted by the exercises of the interior life. Every apostle should have an ardent desire not only to sanctify others, but, first of all, to sanctify himself and to use all the means necessary for this. He should therefore earnestly resolve to use these means; and as mental prayer is the principal and most indispensable of these means, our first and most firm resolution must be this: I will faithfully make mental prayer every morning.

The faithful carrying out of this resolution will be the keystone of the arch of our spiritual edifice and the principal means of securing God's blessing on our apostolic labors. To be a priest, a religious, or even only a simple Christian, how great the dignity, and how grand its ideal! The priest, the religious, and the Christian are each bound, according to his state and dignity, "to put on Jesus Christ" and reproduce in himself His life and virtues, for "as many of you as have been baptized, have put on Christ,"[147] and, therefore, to resemble our divine Savior. Jesus, then, should be the light of our reason, the rule of our actions, both internal and external, and of our affections; our strength in trials, combats, and labors; and the nourishment of our interior life.

But the most indispensable means for forming our interior life after Jesus, our Model, is mental prayer faithfully practiced. Without some practice of mental prayer, we cannot resemble Jesus Christ, for he who is devoid of all good thoughts, of good sentiments, resolutions, and prayers, is surely not on the road to salvation. But he who regularly and faithfully makes mental prayer is protected from every side by an impenetrable armor against his own frailty, the world, and the dangers of his own position.

Father Desurmont, C.SS.R., one of the most experienced conductors of retreats of his time, says that priests and religious must "either make mental prayer or they will be exposed to a great risk of being lost." Cardinal Lavigerie declares that "for an apostolic

---

[147] Gal. 3:27.

laborer, there is no alternative between holiness, at least desired or pursued, and progressive perversion." And the Royal Prophet chants as follows: "O Lord . . . unless Thy law had been my meditation, I had perhaps perished in my abjection; [therefore] Thy justifications I will never forget, for by them, Thou hast given me life."[148]

Priests and religious are to be judged according to their mental prayer. He who faithfully makes his morning meditation, or mental prayer, at the appointed time, and never, without real necessity, omits it, or puts it off to a later hour, and always makes it apart from the prescribed thanksgiving after Mass or Holy Communion, and does not turn it into a preparation for his sermon, and so forth, he, I say, efficaciously desires or tends to holiness. He, however, who acts differently, or does not seriously endeavor to make good meditations, will gradually lapse into that dangerous state of willful tepidity, so displeasing to God, as we can see from the message Jesus sent to the bishop of Laodicea.[149]

In the life of priests and of religious, all their duties are connected together. He who gives up meditation, or omits it willfully, or through carelessness, will soon say Mass and receive Holy Communion without recollection, without fervor, and, therefore, without personal fruits. His recitation of the Divine Office, of vocal prayers, will be only mechanical and burdensome to him and will but feebly express his union with the official prayer of the Church. Such a one will hardly exercise self-watchfulness, the spirit of recollection, and, consequently, will omit brief, spontaneous prayers and spiritual reading. Hence, his apostolate will become always less and less fruitful. Such a one seldom will make any particular examen, or sincerely examine his conscience, or discover his faults

[148] Ps. 118:92-93 (RSV = Ps. 119:92-93).
[149] Apoc. 3:15-16 (RSV = Rev. 3:15-16).

and the dangers to which he is exposed; wherefore, even his confessions also will be wanting in fervor and good results.

❧

What mental prayer is
Prayer is the elevation of the mind to God — not theoretically, but practically, for it is not a mere study, nor made for the purpose of studying, but for the purpose of regulating our conduct. Mental prayer is real work, especially for beginners. It is a work and requires effort for us to detach ourselves, even for a moment, from all that is not God, in order to keep our whole mind and attention fixed on God for a whole half-hour and to take a new start on our way to perfection. Although arduous, if undertaken generously, it will lead to peace in the union and friendship with Jesus. "Mental prayer," says St. Teresa, "is a friendly and intimate communing of the heart with Jesus." In this communing with our loving Jesus, we should speak to Him in the language of faith, hope, and charity, and listen to what He says to us through His inspirations, through our conscience. We should speak to Him in the simple and ingenuous language of a loving child, and make known to Him our misery and desires, our wants, our goodwill, our resolutions, our gratitude, and our sorrow for our sins; and we should offer ourselves to Him to be formed by Him as He wills, and so that He may enable us to please and resemble Him in all out thoughts, words, and actions.

O Lord Jesus,
with Thy most kind and merciful,
and yet most powerful, hand,
deign to form my heart
so that it may be like Thine.

The steps in mental prayer

We should place our reason, and especially our faith and our heart, in the presence of our Lord teaching us a certain truth, or a certain virtue, and should earnestly desire to harmonize our conduct therewith, and then deplore whatever in us is contrary, opposed thereto. And foreseeing certain obstacles in this matter, we should make up our mind to overcome them, but being aware that of ourselves we are powerless to do this, we should pray earnestly for grace to do it effectually.

Let us consider ourselves an exhausted traveler, panting for breath and parched with thirst, looking for a cool spring. At last, *I see* one, but it is on a high, steep rock. *I thirst.* The more I look at that spring, which would so refresh me as to enable me to continue my journey, the more I yearn to quench my increasing thirst. *I will,* cost what it may, reach that spring; and I make every effort, but all in vain. But, there is someone near, who seems to be awaiting my request for help, in order to help me. He even carries me in the steepest places, and after a few minutes, I am able to quench my thirst. In like manner, we can drink of the living waters of grace flowing from the Heart of Jesus.

My evening spiritual reading, which is a very precious element of the interior life, has revived my desire to make tomorrow's mental prayer. Before retiring to rest, I will briefly prepare from my meditation book tomorrow morning's meditation, as well as the fruit I intend to derive from it.

Now the time of my mental prayer has come. I will, as it were, leave this earth, and represent to myself a living and speaking scene to remove all distractions and temporal anxieties. This scene, although rapidly represented, should be striking enough to place me in the presence of God, which should take up all my attention and wholly penetrate me until the end of meditation. In this manner, I am placed near the living, adorable, and lovable Being to converse with Him. Him, then, do I profoundly adore, with humility, sorrow for sin, and protestation of entire dependence, in humble and confiding prayer, that He may bless my communing with Him.

⌒ I see ⌒
Being wholly taken up with Thy living presence,
O my Jesus, and cutting loose, as it were,
from the mere natural order, I am
about to begin my conversation with Thee
in the language of faith, which is more
faithful than the analyses of my reason.
Hence, I will now read the points of my meditation.
Then I will resume them and concentrate my attention thereon.
It is Thou, O Jesus, who speakest to me
and teachest me this truth. I will enliven
and increase my faith concerning this truth,
relying on Thy infinite truth.

And thou, my soul, repeat without ceasing: "I believe this." Again, repeat it still more firmly and, like a child reciting his lesson, repeat many times, that thou adherest to this doctrine and to its consequences for thy eternity:

O Jesus, it is true, absolutely true; I believe it.
I will that this ray of the Sun of Revelation
should serve as my beacon on my journey.
Render my faith still more lively.
Inspire me with an earnest desire to
live according to this ideal and

to detest what is opposed to it.
I wish to assimilate this
truth as my spiritual nourishment.

☞ I thirst ☜

On the frequency and the energy of my acts of faith depend the affections of my heart. These affections are like flowers a childlike heart would cast before Jesus: acts of adoration, gratitude, love, joy, attachment to the divine will and detachment from everything else, hope in God, and self-surrender to Him. My heart chooses one or more of these and deeply penetrates itself therewith, expresses and often repeats them in a loving and sincere manner but in the simplest way. If my feelings are moved, I make use of them, for they may prove useful, although not really necessary. A calm, deep affection is more secure and fruitful than superficial emotions, which do not depend on me and are not an index of a real and fruitful mental prayer. What is always in my power and is especially important is the effort necessary to shake off the torpor of my heart and urge me to say earnestly:

My God, I wish to be united to Thee,
to empty myself before Thee, and give vent to
my gratitude and cheerfully accomplish Thy will.
Henceforth, I wish to tell Thee in all sincerity that
I love Thee and detest all that displeases Thee.

And even when I sincerely try, but my heart
remains cold and is wanting in fervent expressions,
I will acknowledge to Thee, my Jesus,
both my humiliation and my desire,
and will prolong my sorrow for this, with the
hope that Thou wilt graciously accept my desire.

Inner Strength for Active Apostles

O Jesus, how beautiful is the ideal I perceive in Thee.
But is my conduct in harmony with this perfect model?
I examine this point in Thy presence, who seest all things,
who art now all mercy, but wilt be all justice in my particular
judgment, when Thou wilt with a single glance examine
all the actions and the motives of my whole life.
Does my life correspond to this ideal?
Were I to die now, my Jesus, wouldst Thou not find
that my conduct is in opposition to this ideal?

O my good Master, deign to indicate in which
points Thou wishest my amendment.
Help me to find out first the obstacles
that prevent me from imitating Thee,
and then the internal and the external
causes and occasions of my shortcomings.
How do I fulfill my obligations
as a Christian, a religious, a priest?
The commandments of God, the precepts of the
Church, my vows, Mass, Divine Office, prayers,
ministry, labors, charity, the use of my time,
modesty, custody of the senses, behavior in church,
recollection, presence of God, and so forth.
Dost Thou not, O Sacred Heart of Jesus,
require of me more fidelity, more fervor,
more purity of intention, more efforts, more
considerateness, in performing my duties?

The sight of my miseries and difficulties urges me,
O my adorable Redeemer,
to express to Thee my confusion, sorrow, bitter regrets,
and ardent desire to do better and generously and

unreservedly to offer my whole being to Thee,
for I sincerely wish to please Thee in all things.

☞ I will ☜

I am now advancing further into the school of the will. It is the language of charity in effect. The affections have given rise in me to the desire of amendment. I have found out the obstacles, and my will should say, "I will remove them."

O Jesus, my earnestness in saying,
"I will" is a result of my fervor in repeating,
"I believe, I love, I am sorry, I detest."
If at times this "I will" does not come out as
energetically as I would wish, my beloved Savior,
I will deplore the weakness of my will,
and far from getting disheartened,
I will not grow weary repeating how much
I long to participate in Thy generosity in all
that concerns Thy Father's service.

To my general resolution of striving to work out my salvation and to love God, I join the special resolution of applying my mental prayer to this day's difficulties, temptations, and dangers. But I especially have at heart to renew the resolution of my particular examen and strengthen it with motives drawn from our Savior's Heart, and I will indicate the means of fulfilling it, and foresee the occasions for so doing, and prepare for the combats I may have to undergo. If I foresee some special occasion of dissipation of mind, of want of mortification, of humiliation, temptation, or some important matter, I will endeavor to prepare for it by watchfulness, energy, and especially by union with Jesus and recourse to Mary. If, notwithstanding all my precautions, I happen to fall, I will not get discouraged, since I know that God is glorified every time I rise after a fall, but will begin again with renewed fervor, self-diffidence, and self-abasement, to serve Thee more faithfully. It is only by so doing that I can obtain success.

⌒ I will, with Thy help ⌒

St. Augustine says, "It is less absurd to try to compel a lame man to walk straight than to try to succeed without Thee, my Savior." Why have my resolutions remained fruitless? Is it not because the words "I can do all things" are not derived from "in Him who strengtheneth me"?[150] I have now reached that part of my mental prayer, which, under certain aspects, is the most important: the supplication, or the language of hope.

> *Without Thy grace, my Jesus,*
> *I can do nothing, and I am*
> *entirely unable to deserve it.*
> *But I know that my earnest entreaties,*
> *far from wearying Thee, will determine*
> *the measure of Thy help, if they reflect*
> *my ardent desire to be Thine, my self-diffidence,*
> *and my boundless confidence in Thy loving Heart.*
> *Like the Canaanite woman, I prostrate*
> *myself before Thee, O infinite Goodness.*
> *With a persistence, like hers, full of hope*
> *and humility, I beg of Thee, not a few crumbs,*
> *but a real participation in that feast of which Thou*
> *didst say, "My food is to do my Father's will."*[151]

[150] Phil. 4:13.
[151] John 4:34.

Grace having made me a
member of Thy Mystical Body,
I participate in Thy life and merits.
Wherefore, through Thee, my Jesus, I pray,
"Holy Father, I beseech Thee by the Blood of
Thy Son, crying to Thee for mercy for me,"
and Thou canst not reject this my prayer:
"Hear me, O Lord, for I am needy and poor."[152]
Clothe me with Thy strength, and
glorify Thy power in my weakness.
Thy goodness, Thy promises, Thy merits, O Jesus;
my misery and my confidence are my only
claims for obtaining, by my union with Thee,
the custody of my heart and the strength I need this day.
If I meet with some obstacle, temptation, or the necessity of
making some sacrifice, the text or the thought I choose as
my spiritual bouquet will cause me to inhale the
perfume of prayer, which has enveloped my resolutions
and will urge me to raise an efficacious supplication to God.
This habit, as the fruit of my mental prayer,
will also be its touchstone.
"By their fruits you shall know them."[153]

Continue your union with Christ throughout the day
When I shall have made such progress as to live by faith and
by a habitual thirst for God, then only the labor of going through
the "I see" may be sometimes omitted, and the "I thirst" and the

[152] Ps. 85:1 (RSV = Ps. 86:1).
[153] Matt. 7:16.

"I will" will flow forth at the very beginning of the meditation, which will then consist chiefly in producing affections and self-offerings, and in strengthening our firm will, and in beseeching Jesus, directly or through Mary Immaculate, the angels, or the saints, for a more intimate and constant union with the will of God.

Now the holy Sacrifice of the Mass is to take place, and my mental prayer has prepared me for it. My participation in Calvary in the name of the Church, and my holy Communion will be, as it were, a continuation of my mental prayer. During my giving thanks, I will include in my petitions the welfare of the Church, the souls entrusted to me, my labors, relatives, friends, benefactors, the dead, and so forth.

In the course of the day, let us intersperse fervent acts of love of God, spiritual communions, and brief, spontaneous prayers, and strive to make our particular examen, a visit to the Blessed Sacrament and to the Blessed Virgin Mary, to recite five decades of the Rosary, and spend some time in spiritual reading. In this manner, we shall sanctify the whole day and become always more and more united to Jesus.

Chapter Sixteen

Custody of the heart

Our second resolution should regard the custody of our heart, for it is an essential requisite for the apostolate. Hence, let us say, "O Jesus, I am resolved to be habitually solicitous to preserve my heart from every stain, and to unite it always more and more to Thy Heart in all my occupations, conversations, recreations, and so forth." By this resolution, we repudiate all stain, both in the motive and in the execution of our actions. Hence, we must begin our every action with a pure intention and keep up this pure intention during its whole progress. Our ambition, in fact, should be to intensify during its performance the faith, hope, and love animating us. This resolution will be the index of the practical value of our first resolution, for our interior life will be gauged by the custody of our heart, for, says the Holy Spirit, "with all watchfulness keep thy heart, because life issueth out from it."[154]

The custody of the heart enables the traveler to profit by the food he takes before starting on his way or when he stops to rest. It is nothing else than the habitual, or at least the frequent, solicitude to preserve all my acts, in their order, from everything that

[154] Prov. 4:23.

might vitiate or spoil their motive or their performance. Our solicitude should be calm and trustful, since it is based on a childlike recourse to God. It is rather a work of the heart and will than of the mind, which should remain free to perform its part. Far from impeding our action, the custody of the heart perfects it by regulating it according to the spirit of God and adapting it to the duties of our state.

This exercise may be performed at any time by our heart's viewing our present actions and paying moderate attention to the diverse parts of the action we are performing. It is actually putting into practice the maxim "Attend to what thou art doing." Our soul, like a watchful sentinel, exercises its solicitude over all the motions of our heart, over our whole interior, our impressions, intentions, passions, and inclinations, as well as over all our thoughts, words, and deeds. The custody of the heart requires a certain degree of recollection. By frequent exercise, it becomes a habit.

Whither am I going, and for what? How would Jesus act now, were He in my place? What does He now require of me? Such are the questions that come spontaneously to the mind of him who is eager to become an interior man. For the soul that is wont to go to Jesus through Mary, the custody of the heart is more affective, and it becomes an incessant want of his heart to have recourse to Mary. Through her is realized this injunction of Jesus: "Abide in me, and I in you."[155] We can abide in Jesus through Mary's help, and likewise to have Jesus abiding in us. When we invoke Mary, it is because we seek Jesus, for "it is good for me to adhere to my God."[156] In all our labors, we should seek to do God's will, and His will alone; in other words, our only object should be to do God's will.

---

[155] John 15:4.
[156] Ps. 72:28 (RSV = Ps. 73:28).

⌒ Custody of our heart is necessary to us ⌒
My God, *who art holiness itself,*
here below Thou admittest a soul
into Thy intimacy only insofar as
he strives to destroy or shun
every shortcoming, such as spiritual
sloth in raising one's heart to Thee;
an inordinate affection toward creatures;
bluntness, impatience, spite, caprice,
indolence, fondness of ease, and comfort;
facility in speaking without necessity of
the faults of others; dissipation of mind,
vain curiosity; gossip, loquacity, vain
and rash judgments; vain self-complacency;
contempt of others, fault-finding; acting to
draw the esteem and praise of others;
presumption, obstinacy, jealousy,
want of due respect for authority,
and murmurs; and lack of
mortification in eating and drinking.
What a swarm of venial sins,
or of willful imperfections,
which will take possession of me
if I neglect to watch over myself,
and which shall deprive me of the graces
Thou hast reserved for me from all eternity!
If I fail to combat them, they will be apt to paralyze
and sterilize all my spiritual exercises and good works!

Let us not deceive ourselves by imagining that all these are
faults of mere human frailty; but let us in all earnestness watch

over ourselves, that we may avoid them and correct them. "The Kingdom of heaven suffereth violence, and the violent bear it away."[157]

◦ Custody of the heart is based on
the exercise of the presence of God ◦
O most Holy Trinity,
if, as I hope, I am in the state of grace,
Thou dwellest in my heart with all Thy
glory and Thy infinite perfections,
although hidden to me under the veil of faith.
Every moment, Thou seest me and all that I do
Thy mercy and Thy justice incessantly operate in me.
To punish my faults, Thou at times withdrawest
Thy choice graces from me, or Thou ceasest to dispose
in a maternal manner, for my benefit, certain events,
and sometimes Thou loadest me with fresh benefits.
If I really considered Thy indwelling in me as
most important to me and most worthy of my
attention, would I think so seldom thereon and
fail so often in my duty of self-watchfulness?
My spontaneous prayers,
following each other in quick succession,
should have recalled to me this
all-loving indwelling of God in me.
Have I even marked every hour of the
day by some pious aspiration?
And what place do my spiritual communions
occupy in my daily actions?

[157] Matt. 11:12.

142

And nevertheless, my God,
Thou art ready at every
moment to listen to me,
to remind me of Thy indwelling in me,
and to strengthen it by the infusion of
fresh graces of the Redemption in my soul.
What profit have I hitherto derived from
all these treasures placed within my reach?
How far I am from being one of those
souls who, while attending to their tasks
and to those who are with them,
many and many times each day turn
their thoughts and affection to Him
who is their Guest, their Treasure!
"Where thy treasure is,
there also is thy heart."[158]

⌁ Devotion to our Lady
facilitates custody of the heart ⌁
O Mary,
my Immaculate Mother,
thy divine Son on Calvary
made me thy child, in order
that thou shouldst help me to
guard my heart united by Jesus
to the Blessed Trinity.
I purpose to invoke Thee always
more and more frequently to
help me to purify my heart and all its

[158] Matt. 6:21.

propensities, intentions,
affections, and desires.
I will henceforth heed
thy interior admonitions
to avoid whatever may not
be pleasing to God.
Often remind me to
consider before acting:
What is my real
intention in doing this?
What would Jesus do in my place?

How to practice custody of the heart

I regret so long losing sight of the presence of God during my occupations, as well as the many faults that then escape me, and the danger of tepidity to which they expose me. Hence, I am resolved at once to begin to practice custody of the heart. Hence, in my morning meditation, I will designate a special time during my work, when, without in the least neglecting my duty, I will recall most vividly God's presence to my mind and raise my heart to Him in love and interior prayer. A similar exercise of four or five minutes I will begin to practice morning and evening in the most fervent manner possible.

This will serve as an apprenticeship to the interior life; it is a kind of spiritual retreat, short, indeed, but very efficacious, for, says St. Francis de Sales, "In the exercise of spiritual retreat and aspirations lies the great work of devotion. This exercise can supply the lack of all other prayers, but its want can hardly be repaired by any other means. Without it, we can but ill perform the duties of the active life."

This exercise will enable us to discover all the interior motives we have for our actions, to correct what may be amiss therein, to purify our intention and act as Jesus would do in our place, to confide lovingly in Jesus, and to ask Him for the help we need. Let us not fail at night, during our examination of conscience, to examine carefully how we have performed this exercise, and to impose on ourselves some salutary penance, in case we have omitted it or performed it carelessly. If we faithfully perform it every day, we shall soon experience its marvelous results and draw God's blessing on ourselves and our labors. We shall then be able to do what God wills, as He wills, and because He wills it, and our life will be, as it were, transformed, and our hearts will be united to Jesus.

Part Six

The priest's liturgical life

Chapter Seventeen

⁓

A priest's resolution
concerning his liturgical life

I am resolved to live as my Mass, my Divine Office, and my other liturgical functions require; that is, I will not merely "go through them," or fittingly perform them, but I will perform them so as to render them profitable to my interior life through Jesus, with Jesus, and in Jesus, and to exercise my zeal for the praise and service of God in the name of the Church.

If the truths taught concerning the Holy Sacrifice of the Mass but feebly impress my mind and my faith, if each Mass does not clothe me more thoroughly with Jesus Christ by inspiring me with a horror of sin, with humility, with the spirit of sacrifice, with love of God, and with ardent zeal for His glory, it is certain that I do not live my Mass. Nor do I live my Divine Office, if each of its hours does not bring back to my mind the thought of the Holy Sacrifice and urge me to fulfill this admonition of St. Paul: "Let this mind be in you, which was also in Christ Jesus."[159] I do not live my liturgical functions, all of which contain a deep symbolic meaning, if I do not realize that the Church intends them to adopt men's souls to

---

[159] Phil. 2:5.

the sacraments, and to enable them to maintain and increase the life of Jesus in souls, and also to increase in me the life of Jesus. If I am of a truly liturgical spirit, I shall so perform these functions as to edify all assisting at them.

Reasons for this resolution

Pope Pius X says, "The active participation in the holy mysteries and in the public and solemn prayers of the Church is the first and indispensable source of the true Christian spirit." Besides the morning meditation, which teaches us that "it behooves that Jesus should reign over us,"[160] we should, during the day, "watch and pray, lest we enter into temptation."[161] And "it behooveth always to pray and not faint,"[162] lest we fall into numerous venial faults. The Liturgy of the Church is a powerful means of avoiding sin and making progress in the interior life, for it keeps us in frequent communion with Jesus and under His influence and protection.

The Mass, the Divine Office and the other liturgical functions enrich us spiritually by promoting in us piety, the spirit of prayer, and union with God, and should preserve us from performing our priestly functions through the mere force of habit, as if they were a trade, a mere means of earning a living, or with only natural intentions. Our spiritual life should be animated with piety; otherwise our life would not resemble that of Christ, and would be but natural and devoid of all that is supernatural. Our Mass, Divine Office, and our other liturgical functions, being intended by God and His Church as means of promoting our sanctification, should increase

[160] 1 Cor. 15:25.
[161] Cf. Matt. 26:41.
[162] Cf. Luke 18:1.

our spiritual life and enable us to spend ourselves generously for souls, without detriment to ourselves. But without mental prayer, our liturgical life would be too speculative, and would have but little, if any, practical influence over our progress in the spiritual life, for, says Jesus Christ, "not everyone that saith to me, 'Lord, Lord,' shall enter into the kingdom of Heaven."[163] "Without mental prayer," says Pius X, "priests will perform their sacred functions coldly, carelessly, and perhaps even unworthily."[164]

We should not consider the Divine Office as a burden, but as a nourishment of our piety, an adjunct to mental prayer. We should study its meaning, influence, and usefulness, and seek to develop in ourselves the liturgical sense. At our ordination, the bishop said to us, "Recognize what you are doing; imitate what you are handling."

That priest leads a liturgical life who knows how to make use of the Mass, the Divine Office, and his official rites to increase his union with the Church, to make progress in the interior life and thereby more perfectly to reflect the virtues of Christ in the sight of the faithful. It is in the very bosom of the Most Holy Trinity that we should contemplate the eternal liturgy, by which the three Divine Persons chant the divine life in the ineffable hymn of the generation of the Word and the procession of the Holy Spirit. The Incarnation is the substantial and living association of the whole work of God, the Creation and the Redemption, with that Liturgy. The Incarnate Word longs for the glorification of His Father and the diffusion of His Spirit. To excite this longing in men's souls is the object of the Liturgy of the Church. An individual man, when he is isolated, can but very feebly glorify God; but when he is united to the whole Church by the Communion of Saints, he

---

[163] Matt. 7:21.
[164] *Haerent Animo.*

enters, as a power of praise, into the infinite, as it were, for he becomes one with all who chant the praises of the Blessed Trinity, that is, with the Lamb of God and Sun of the heavenly Jerusalem, the choirs of angels, the court of the elect, the souls in Purgatory, and the Church Militant. Therefore, his voice is united with the Divine Persons as well as with all creation, and the exercise of praise becomes an official and, as it were, a divine act.

The Church, being the Spouse of Jesus, whose life is supereminently one of adoration, reparation, thanksgiving, and supplication, transmits to the priest's soul the sentiments and even the very expressions imparted to her by the Incarnate Word directing her, and thus, the Liturgy on earth becomes one with the eternal liturgy of the Most Holy Trinity. An isolated drop of water is but little more than nothing, but when united to the ocean, it participates in its power and immensity.

The same happens to the soul praying through Jesus Christ, in union with the Church. The soul's prayer thus becomes divine, as it were, and embraces all ages, from the creation of the angels and their first adoration, to our own time; from Adam and his familiar conversation in the earthly Paradise with the Creator; from the offerings of Abel, Melchisedech, and Abraham, the prayers and penances of David and the other saints of the Old Law down to Calvary, the center of the Liturgy, and the Eucharist, its loving memorial. It comprises all the generations of holy souls whom the Church has brought forth since Pentecost. But we should, moreover, bear in mind, that this prayer (Liturgy) is identified through the Divine Word and the Holy Spirit, with the eternal praises unceasingly issuing from the furnace of infinite Love, the Most Holy Trinity.

The liturgical soul participates more and more in the life and virtues of Jesus Christ, first, by perfecting the communion of the soul with God, for it increases in it the habit, or virtue, of religion and develops the chief elements of the spiritual life; and second, it associates the soul, through the cycle of the feasts, with all the renewed phases of our Savior's earthly life, such as His eucharistic and glorious life, and imparts simplicity, attractiveness and efficacy to the habitual exercise of charity, the mother and queen of all virtues. The virtue of religion places us in relation with God. By the Mass, our divine Savior instituted the greatest and holiest of sacrifices, the greatest act of religion dominating on earth whatever unites the creature to the Creator. The Church unites us to or fits us for this Sacrifice, by prescribing the rites of the sacraments, instituting the sacramentals and arranging the words, chants, acts, and rubrics that constitute the Liturgy.

The object of the virtue of religion is, as its name implies, to bind man again to God[165] by inducing him to give due worship to God, his Creator and Father. It develops in us the need of calling to mind the divine presence and the fundamental spirit of adoration, which inspires us with sentiments of the deepest humility before the Divine Majesty and causes us to offer Him our filial and unreserved homage. Jesus Christ declared that His mission was to form "true adorers of the Father in spirit and in truth."[166] He Himself is the prototype and model of these adorers and therefore personifies the virtue of religion. Only the theological virtues are superior to the virtue of religion, for it is the most excellent of the moral virtues, being directly concerned with the worship of God. Devotion is its most essential act. It enables us to turn the regret of our unfaithfulness to God into contrition, and the thought of God's benefits into spiritual joys.

[165] The word *religion* comes from the Latin *religare*, "to bind again."
[166] John 4:23.

The virtue of religion disposes our soul for the gift of piety, which is so essential to the spiritual life, for, says St. Paul, "Piety is profitable to all things, having promise of the life that now is, and of that which is to come."[167] Piety is also the base of the science of prayer.

❧

Four fruits are acquired through the Liturgy

The Liturgy may be considered a school for acquiring four fruits: the presence of God, sorrow for sin, joy, and prayer.

• *The presence of God.* With admirable abundance and variety, the Liturgy reminds us of the dogma of the Blessed Trinity; and this mystery, by revealing to us God's essential and intimate life, recalls our beginning and our final end and, consequently, God's eternal life and the immortality of our soul. The liturgical soul lives by the thought of eternity and, in the light of eternity, disposes its existence and reanimates its filial fear and its firm confidence in God and His Providence over all things. The soul, being so frequently reminded of the worship of God and His infinite perfections, acquires a habitual attitude of reverence and adoration toward God. Being thus in the presence of God, the Rewarder of the good and Punisher of the wicked, the soul acquires a filial and cheerful obedience and submission in all things to His divine will, and a profound respect for God's rights and dispensations.

• *Sorrow for sin.* Fidelity to the divine law is the measure of participation in the divine life. The Liturgy constantly recalls this truth to the priest's conscience, for its themes are unfaithfulness, or sin, the consequences of sin, its hideousness, death, its

---

[167] Cf. 1 Tim. 4:8.

punishment, the certainty of death, the uncertainty of death, and its eternal consequences. Calvary and the altar, placed between Heaven and earth, enable us to acquire a happy eternity and give us the means of repairing our offenses against the Divine Majesty. All this exerts a most beneficent influence over the soul living by the Liturgy. That soul, united to the satisfaction the Man-God gave for sin, repairs his offenses by a sincere sorrow, deep indeed, yet calm, confiding, and childlike. Father Faber calls this sorrow the touchstone of devotion, and a true sign of a healthy soul in those who experience the need of sorrow and pray for it.

• *Joy.* Devotion nourished by the Liturgy soon becomes a habit and makes the faithful priest conscious of being an adopted son of God, a brother, a friend, and a minister of Jesus Christ, and a temple of the Holy Spirit. This will enable him to acquire not only the peace surpassing all understanding,[168] but also a spiritual joy, experienced even amid sore trials and sufferings, and causing him "to run in the way of God's commandments."[169] Schooled by the Breviary, the liturgical soul becomes a eucharistic soul, for it was after the Last Supper that Jesus said to His Apostles, "These things I have spoken to you, that my joy may be in you, and your joy may be filled."[170] In the same school, the soul acquires a deep and strong devotion to the Blessed Virgin Mary, whom the Church rightly calls the "cause of our joy."

• *Prayer.* He truly knows how to live well, who knows how to pray well, for, says St. Augustine, "the great science of life is the science of prayer." In the Liturgy we find prayers adapted to every

---

[168] Phil. 4:7.
[169] Cf. Ps. 118:32 (RSV = Ps. 119:32).
[170] John 15:11.

situation and circumstance in life. To him who lives his Mass, Breviary, and ritual, so great a variety of resourceful prayers is offered that he will find therein in every circumstance and want the necessary means to raise him to God, to praise him, and to implore mercy and help. St. Alphonsus preferred one prayer of the Divine Office to a hundred private prayers. Louis Veuillot[171] acknowledged that assisting in a church when the 118th Psalm in the "Little Hours" was recited in choir had a wonderful effect in reanimating his devotion.

• How consoling to the priest reciting the Divine Office is the assurance that he is praying as God wills, and that he is praying not alone, but with and through the Church, and in the name of the Church.

*The priest must habitually
exercise the virtue of charity*

By means of the Incarnation, God intended to satisfy the need we feel of possessing Him in a visible manner, in order the more easily to love Him. This is what the Church means by chanting in the Preface of Christmas, "That whilst we visibly know God, we may be drawn through Him to love things invisible." "Love," says St. Thomas, "is nourished both by the presence of the Beloved, which enables us to have a more intimate perception of his lovableness, and by the proofs of love which he gives us."

• *Jesus present to us.* The Incarnation, the descent of the Divine Life in our midst, is the most striking manifestation of God's ineffable love for each of us. By means of the Holy Sacrifice of the

---

[171] Louis Veuillot (1813-1883), French journalist and writer.

altar, of His Church, His Gospel, and the Sacraments, our Emmanuel continues to live among us, and to give us proofs of His inexhaustible love. Along with preaching, the Liturgy adapts souls for participating in the Divine Life, and does even more. In order to render our participation efficacious and continuous, the Liturgy explains and transfers to us the manifestation of this life of Jesus Christ in our midst, and keeps us in the atmosphere of Jesus. It speaks to us and enables us also to speak the language of our amiable Savior, thus continuing, as it were, our Lord's living among us, rendering Him ever present to us, atoning for us, praying and acting with us, and presenting Himself to us to manifest to us His infinite lovableness.

• *Jesus proves His love.* Love and sacrifice are inseparable. Wherefore, everything in Jesus gravitates around His Cross. Everything in the Liturgy gravitates also around the Mass, the living chart of the proofs of the love of Jesus for each of us. Our Savior's whole life, says Bossuet, is summed up in the spirit of sacrifice. Wherefore, everything in the Liturgy tends to cause the priest to correspond to the love of Jesus by a spirit of immolation, which is a feature of love. All the varieties and degrees of love are taught in the school of the Liturgy, such as the love of hope, of complacency, of benevolence, and of preference, which penetrate into the soul through the admirable collects, psalms, prayers for the living and the dead, blessings, consecrations, ceremonies, and so forth.

• *Union with Jesus.* It is Jesus Himself who continues His great lesson of love. The Liturgy represents Him to us as one we live with, and shows Him to us as the object, the term, and the model of our love. Through the Eucharist, He has been and remains the proof of what love demands and offers us unceasing opportunities to enable us to return love for love to Him.

The shepherd in Landes, France, crossing his swampy fields, has to look where he places his stilts; he is an image of those who, having a task to perform, are absorbed by its difficulty. On the other hand, the bird, coming to the same swamps to seek its food, scarcely skims over their surface. Such also is the priest who knows how to profit by the Liturgy; he always more and more takes as his motto the saying of the early Christians: "Christ is my life."[172] By his union with Jesus, he can escape all hostile snares, for he can say with the psalmist, "He shall pluck my feet out of the snare" and, "My eyes are always fixed on the Lord."[173]

⋄ *Everything for the Mass.* For the priest endowed with the liturgical understanding, the sacrifice of Calvary is ever present to him, and everything brings him back to it. When he has to perform a heroic act of detachment, as some painful duty, a suffering, or an insult to bear, he first sees Jesus claiming that sacrifice from him as a proof of his love; wherefore, he finds therein but little difficulty, if any. For a priest who is convinced that Jesus lives in His Church and in each one of the faithful, religion is something more than a mere summary of doctrines and laws binding us again to God, for it is Christ offering Himself, living in His Mystical Body, everywhere present and demanding us to reciprocate His love. "I set always the Lord in my sight, for He is at my right hand, that I be not moved."[174] And even when he is bruised by the trial, he is not sad, for he has found support and consolation, because Jesus is there, who suffered and immolated Himself, and wishes to continue in the priest His life of suffering.

---

[172] Cf. Phil. 1:21.
[173] Cf. Ps. 24:15 (RSV = Ps. 25:15).
[174] Ps. 15:8 (RSV = Ps. 16:8).

• *Through Him.* Everything happens to the priest through Christ. Through Jesus he goes to the Father, receives the vivifying sap imparting life to him in every form, especially through sacrifice. Through Jesus he acts, because in all things he follows the spirit of Jesus, whom he endeavors to imitate.

• *With Him.* The Emmanuel everywhere accompanies him; the altar, the sacraments, the Divine Office, dyed with the Blood of the Lamb, maintain him in the company of Jesus and facilitate the custody of his heart near the Heart of Him whom he adores, thanks, or implores, and from whom he now hears the calls of grace.

• *In Him.* For him, the spiritual combat, the practice of virtue, and trials lose all that is painful and repulsive in them, for, says Monsignor Gay, "The cross is enlivened and becomes the crucifix, and love is now in its place." In fact, it is Jesus visiting him therein and inviting him to immolate himself. To the priest who lives his Mass, Divine Office, and ritual, duties, sufferings, and humiliation now appear in their true light, as most affectionate marks of friendship of the divine Heart of Jesus. And if a tendency to tepidity arises in the liturgical priest, the Judge present, to preserve in His love him who is consecrated to Him, fills him with a dread of yielding.

The priest's knowledge of his duties, of the practice of the virtues, may prove useful to him, but his progress in the interior life will be owing rather to his liturgical life and mental prayer. So long as he is faithful to them, Jesus is his prudence, His tactics, his strength and constancy, and for him the examination of conscience and the practice of mortification will be exercises of love. To such a priest we may apply the saying of Jesus to St. Catherine of Siena:[175] "Thy measure shall be mine." These words

---

[175] St. Catherine of Siena (1347-1380), Dominican tertiary.

are a commentary on this passage of the Imitation: "Thy progress shall be proportionate to the violence thou dost to thyself."[176] The measure of Jesus is to repay a hundredfold the slightest proofs of love shown Him. How grand the reward of the spirit of sacrifice!

• *The glory of God.* Because the praises of God hold an important place in the Liturgy, the priest is naturally led to connect his personal sanctification directly with his zeal for God's glory. In the Psalms especially, the liturgical soul unites itself to the reparative life of Calvary and the altar, and the many souls who know well how greatly sin is opposed to the divine glory offer themselves as victims of reparation for sin in union with Jesus crucified.

• *Union with Heaven.* The faithful priest loves to contemplate the divine glory at the altar, but especially in Heaven. This he does eagerly, not only by the oft-repeated doxologies of the Mass and the Divine Office, but also by his own habitual and intimate union with the Divine Dweller in the tabernacle, for the living Heart of Jesus in the ciborium is the same that radiates in the elect and secures them in the consummation of love by the vision and possession of God. The faithful priest can truly say with St. Paul, "Our conversation is in Heaven."[177] For him, Heaven is no longer an inaccessible region. He proceeds from the mystery of the Cross and the life of which the Sacred Host is the source, to the fundamental devotion of the Blessed Trinity. These two principal thoughts in the Liturgy combine with the Communion of Saints and form that of our heavenly country. Consequently, the cycle of the feasts of Easter, of the Blessed Virgin, and of the saints impart to the priest leading a liturgical life a real homesickness for his

---

[176] Thomas à Kempis, *Imitation of Christ,* Bk. 1, ch. 25.
[177] Phil. 3:20.

heavenly home, which Pope St. Gregory considers as a proof of the state of grace and a guarantee of predestination.

⌒

Four practical means of realizing our resolution
I now renew, and this more precisely, my resolution to be a liturgical soul, in order to be more intimately united with Thee, O Jesus, and thereby to render my apostolate more fruitful.

The more my intimate life gravitates around the Divine Office and the holy Sacrifice of the Mass, the more will Jesus reign in me. By an interior life I will glorify God and the apostolate so much as the altar shall be the source of my devotedness, my sacrifices, my confidence, and my official and private prayer. The liturgical words and rites shall powerfully assist me to live the great divine praise, to derive greater profit from the Precious Blood, and to put on Jesus Christ. When in danger of sinning, I will make use of the fear of God to preserve me therefrom. With the help derived from the Liturgy, I will sacrifice myself wholly and unreservedly to God, in union with the Sacrifice of Calvary incessantly renewed on the altar, and by my vigilance and efforts, I will succeed to cause Jesus to reign in me.

By the custody of my heart I will render my voice more pure and less unworthy of being associated with the prayers of the Church ascending heavenward to God, through supplication and immolation. Wherefore, the object of my liturgical life, the most noble life to which a human creature can aspire, is union with God by the efficacious, universal, and loving reign of Jesus in me. But with regard to the apostolate, the object of my liturgical life is to live more perfectly my share of the social life of the Church.

For this object, the Lord wishes, first, that I should, especially through the Liturgy, form my intimate life according to the life of

Inner Strength for Active Apostles

Jesus, in order to train my faculties in a generous dependence on God. If I exercise my apostolate through liturgical functions, my preaching and my works, both domestic and social, shall flow from them as from their cause. In this way, I shall become more and more a child of the Church, a member of Christ, and an apostle worthy of God, who can truly say with St. Paul, "Christ liveth in me."

⌒ The liturgical formation ⌒
O good Master,
give me a high esteem for the
Liturgy and a holy eagerness to
develop my liturgical understanding
and thus enlarge my soul's horizon.
I will devote a portion of my reading
to the study and consideration of the
subjects and feasts of the Liturgy so as
to derive spiritual profit from them.
This will help me, by means of mental
prayer, to acquire purity, self-denial, the
spirit of prayer, and a perfect control over
my imagination and my senses and all the
dispositions necessary to derive profit from
the Liturgy and increase my union with God;
and I shall then be able to say Mass and recite
the Divine Office worthily, attentively,
and devoutly without great effort.

⌒ The time to be spent ⌒
"Hurry," says St. Francis de Sales speaking of the Divine Office and of holy Mass, "kills devotion." I should, therefore, devote a whole half-hour to saying Mass, so that not only the Canon but all

its parts may nourish my piety. This is also the teaching of St. Alphonsus. Therefore, I will disregard all the pretexts that Satan may suggest with regard to apostolic zeal, in order to induce me to hurry my Mass, and I will make due reparation for the faults I may commit in this important matter. I will avoid all hurry also in all other liturgical functions.

As for the Divine Office, I will fix a time for its recitation; and at the time appointed, I will at once interrupt, or lay aside, every other occupation, and I am determined that my recitation of it shall be as a prayer from my inmost heart.

> O my Jesus, inspire me with a
> horror of all hurry and carelessness,
> whenever I represent Thee,
> or act in the name of the Church,
> for "cursed is he who doth the work
> of God fraudulently [precipitately]."[178]

⌁ The preparation ⌁

"Before prayer, prepare thy soul."[179] The whole life of Jesus was a preparation for His Sacrifice on the Cross. Hence, our daily (morning) meditation should be a preparation for our Mass. This serious thought: "I shall soon be in contact with the living Love itself," should stir up our fervor and preserve us from all carelessness and precipitation.

Immediately before Mass and before our Divine Office, we should reawaken a deep and energetic act of recollection. Father Olivaint, S.J., was wont to say, "I make my meditation well, so that

[178] Cf. Jer. 48:10.
[179] Ecclus. 18:23 (RSV = Sir. 18:23).

I may say my Mass properly; and I say my Mass and the Divine Office properly, in order to make a good meditation on the following day."

May the spirit of faith take possession of my
mind and heart, so that, being intimately
convinced of the presence of the heavenly spirits
at my Mass and Divine Office, "I will sing to Thee,
my God, in the sight of the angels."[180]
Deign therefore to inspire me with the reverential
awe, with which even Mary deigns to address Thee!

I am one with our Mediator, Jesus, and one with the Church as her representative. This requires me to be devout and dignified, and to avoid hurry and levity in all my priestly functions. I will always be mindful of the words the bishop addressed to me at my ordination: "Recognize what you are doing; imitate what you are handling."

⁀ Celebration and recitation ⁀

If I thus prepare myself to celebrate Mass and to recite the Divine Office, my whole being will concur in representing and glorifying Jesus, the eternal Priest: my body, by its respectful attitude, the exact pronunciation of the words, somewhat more slowly in the principal parts, and the careful observance of the rubrics; my mind, in choosing from the words and rites whatever is apt to nourish my heart; the tone of my voice, and the manner in which I make the Sign of the Cross and the genuflections will manifest, not only that I am aware of Him whom I am addressing, of what I am saying to Him, and what kind of an apostolate I am exercising,

[180] Ps. 137:1 (RSV = Ps. 138:1).

but also whether it is my faith that is prompting me. I am resolved to say Mass like St. Vincent de Paul and St. Alphonsus, who said Mass so devoutly as to cause the assistants to say of each of them, "How well and edifyingly does this priest say Mass!" Hence, I will never say Mass, or perform any priestly function, so carelessly and hurriedly as to occasion in the minds of those present doubts concerning my faith!

When saying Mass and the Divine Office, we may sometimes attend to the meaning of the words, to each word in particular, or briefly meditate on a word or sentence that impresses us. I will then follow the counsel of St. Bernard: "Our mind should agree with our voice." At other times, the mystery of the feast, or some other pious thought may rivet our attention throughout, or only for a moment. During the Canon of the Mass and the Consecration, we may offer ourselves in sacrifice to Jesus, so that as He is on the altar "tanquam agnus occisus," we may unite ourselves to Him in a spirit of sacrifice. And during the day, let us be patient and generous in our labors, crosses, and difficulties for His sake, out of a spirit of penance.

Chapter Eighteen

~

Devotion to Mary is necessary to the priest

The priest — in fact, every apostle — stands in need of an ardent devotion to the Immaculate Virgin Mary. He should take St. Bernard as his model in this; for nearly half a century, St. Bernard exercised the apostolate among monarchs and nations, in assemblies and councils and with the Pope. Exalted by all for his holiness, his genius, his deep knowledge of Scripture, and the penetrating unction of his sermons, and revered in the Church as the "Last of the Fathers," he is, moreover, the chanter of Mary, of her power and mercy, and of her glories. He furnishes matter for the praises of Mary to subsequent writers, to prove that all divine graces and favors come to us through Mary:

> Brethren, let us consider with what sentiments of devotion God wishes us to honor Mary, for He has placed in her the fullness of every good. If we have any hope, any grace or pledge of salvation, let us acknowledge that it all comes to us from her who superabounds in delights.
>
> If the sun, which imparts light to the world, were taken away, all light would disappear on earth. Take away Mary,

the Star of the sea, of our great and vast ocean, and what will remain but a deep obscurity, the shadow of death, and a dense darkness. Wherefore, it behooves us to honor Mary from our inmost heart, for such is the will of Him who willed that we should obtain all we need through Mary. Wherefore, whatever the apostolic man does for his salvation and spiritual progress, and for the fecundity of his apostolate, will rest on a foundation of sand unless it rests on a very special devotion to our Lady.

For, if the apostle, in his interior life, is not sufficiently devoted to Mary, his spiritual Mother, if his confidence in her lacks enthusiasm, if his homage to her is merely external, he will never sanctify himself. Like Jesus, her Son, who beholds the heart, Mary regards only our heart, and looks upon us as her true children, only when the strength of our love corresponds to hers. We should be firmly convinced of the incomparable grandeurs, privileges, and functions of her who is the Mother of God and the Mother of men. We should be fully persuaded that our combats against our defects, the acquisition of the virtues, the reign of Jesus Christ in our soul, and, consequently, all security of salvation and sanctification are proportionate to a degree of our devotion to Mary, and that, when we act with or through Mary, everything in our interior life becomes easier, securer, and sweeter and is much sooner attained.

Our heart should overflow with childlike confidence in her in every occurrence, and we shall experience her considerateness, kind attentions, tender love, mercy, and generosity. "Mary," says St. Bernard, "is my greatest security, the whole base of my hope." Our heart should be inflamed with love for her, our Mother, for she shares our joys, our trials. Let us listen to the beautiful words of St. Bernard:

Devotion to Mary is necessary to the priest

O thou, who feelest thyself tossed by tempests amid the shoals of the sea of this world, turn not away thine eyes from the Star of the sea, if thou wouldst avoid shipwreck. If the winds of temptation blow, if tribulations rise up like rocks before thee, cast a look at the Star, heave a sigh toward Mary. If the waves of pride, ambition, calumny, and jealousy seek to swallow up thy soul, turn thine eyes toward the Star, breathe a prayer to Mary. If anger and love of pleasure threaten thy frail bark, seek the protecting look of Mary. If horror of thine own sins, remorse of conscience, and dread of the divine judgments overwhelm thee with sadness, seeking to plunge thee into the abyss of despair, cling closely to Mary. In thy dangers, in thy anguish, in thy doubts think of Mary, call on Mary. Let the sweet name of Mary be on thy lips, in thy heart; and whilst seeking the assistance of her prayers, lose not the sight of her example, of her virtues. So long as thou followest her, thou canst not go astray. So long as thou invokest her, thou canst not be without hope. So long as thou thinkest on her, thou wilt remain in the right path. So long as she sustains thee, thou canst not fall. So long as she protects thee, thou hast nothing to fear. If she favors thy voyage, thou shalt reach the harbor of safety without exhaustion.

Blessed Grignon de Montfort[181] says, "With Mary we make in one month more progress in the love of Jesus, than we could make in many, were we less united to our good Mother."

[181] St. Louis de Montfort (1673-1716), founder of the Sisters of the Divine Wisdom and the Missionary Priests of Mary who is known for his book *True Devotion to Mary*. He was canonized in 1947, many years after this book was written.

In the second place, whether the apostle has to draw souls out of sin, or to cause the virtues to flourish in them, it behooves him, like St. Paul, to have as his first object to cause Jesus Christ to live in them. But, as Bossuet declares, God having determined to give us Jesus Christ through Mary, will not change the order He laid down, because He is unchangeable. Mary, therefore, in accordance with this order, having given birth to Jesus Christ, the Head of the Mystical Body of the Church, has also to give birth to its members. To isolate Mary from the apostolate would be to misunderstand an essential part of the divine plan of salvation. Hence St. Augustine says, "All the predestined in this world are hidden, guarded, nourished and grow in the bosom of this good Mother, until she brings them forth to glory after their death." "Since the Incarnation," says St. Bernardine of Siena,[182] "Mary has acquired a kind of jurisdiction over the temporal mission of the Holy Spirit, so that no creature receives grace except through her hands."

But he who is devoted to Mary becomes, in his turn, all-powerful over the heart of Mary, his Mother. Consequently, no true apostle should entertain any doubt as to the efficacy of his apostolate if he has a true devotion to Mary, for he will be able to dispose of Mary's omnipotent power over the Blood of the Redeemer. Experience confirms this, for all who have effected numerous conversions of sinners have been most devoted servants of Mary. How great and persuasive are the words and prayers of Mary's devout clients, when they labor to draw souls out of sin, for they are as if identified with the Immaculate Virgin by their horror of sin and their love of holy purity. It was at the sound of Mary's voice that the Precursor

---

[182] St. Bernardine of Siena (1380-1444), popular preacher and reformer of the Franciscan Order who spread devotion to the Holy Name of Jesus

recognized the presence of Jesus Christ and leaped for joy. And what wonderful power have the words of the intimate servants of the Mother of Mercy to prevent despair from seizing those who have long abused grace! How admirably successful is the apostle, who is devoted to Mary, in moving hardened sinners to repentance and perfect conversion through Mary!

Mary living in the heart of the apostle is the very eloquence that enables him to move powerfully souls hitherto unmoved! Jesus seems, by an admirable delicacy, to reserve to His Mother's meditation the most difficult conquests of the apostolate, and to grant them to her devoted servants, so that we may truly say, "Through them He hath reduced our foes to naught."[183] We apostles should most tenderly love her, whom Pius IX called "The Virgin Priest," whose dignity excels that of priests and pontiffs. This love empowers us never to look upon as lost the work we have begun with Mary, and are willing to continue with her, that is, in a manner pleasing to her. Mary, in fact, is at the base and at the crowning point of every work that interests the glory of God through His divine Son.

But let us beware of imagining that we are working with Mary, if we limit ourselves to raising altars in her honor, or in having hymns sung in her praise. What Mary requires of us is a devotedness which enables us to assert in all sincerity, that we habitually live united to her and have recourse to her as the Mother of Good Counsel, that we strive to please her, and that all our prayers to God are made through her intercession. Let us, however, be assured that Mary expects of us a devotion which will cause us to imitate the virtues we admire in her, and surrender ourselves into her hands, that she may enable us "to put on Jesus Christ."[184]

[183] Cf. Jth. 13:22.
[184] Rom. 13:14.

St. Alphonsus's prayer for zeal

O my Lord Jesus Christ,
how can I thank Thee enough for having
called me to the same work Thou
didst Thyself on earth — that is,
to labor for the salvation of souls?
How have I deserved this honor, this reward
after having so grievously offended Thee,
and caused others also to do so?
Thou dost, indeed, O my Lord,
call me to help Thee in this great undertaking.
I will serve Thee with all my strength.
Behold, I offer Thee all my labor,
and even my blood, in order to obey Thee.
Nor do I by this aspire to gratify my
own inclination, or to gain applause or esteem;
I desire nothing else than to see Thee
loved by all men as Thou deservest.
I prize my happy lot and consider myself
fortunate in having been chosen by Thee
for this great work, in which I protest

that I will renounce all the praises
of men and all self-satisfaction,
and will seek only Thy glory.

To Thee be all the honor and satisfaction,
and to me only all the hardships,
the blame, and the reproaches.
Accept, O Lord, this offering that I,
a miserable sinner, who wish to love Thee
and to see Thee loved by others,
make of myself to Thee,
and give me strength to execute it.

Most holy Mary, my advocate,
who so greatly lovest souls, help me. Amen.

Jean-Baptiste Chautard

(1858-1935)

Jean-Baptiste Chautard entered the Cistercian Fraternity at Aiguebelle, France, at the age of nineteen. In 1897, he was elected Abbot of Chambarand, and from 1899 until his death, he served as Abbot of Sept-Fons. He also directed several other Cistercian monasteries. Dom Chautard is perhaps best known for his writings on the apostolate, whose fruitfulness, he emphasizes, depends on a deep interior life.